Lovers, Doctors, and the Law

Lovers, Doctors, and the Law

Your Legal Rights and Responsibilities
in Today's Sex-Health Crisis

Margaret L. Davis, J.D.

In Consultation with Robert S. Scott, M.D.

PERENNIAL LIBRARY

Harper & Row, Publishers, New York
Cambridge, Philadelphia, San Francisco, Washington
London, Mexico City, São Paulo, Singapore, Sydney

For my mother and father

A special thanks to my editor, Janet Goldstein, for her commitment and direction, and to Louis Alexander, Stewart Perry, and Mark Scherzer for their legal expertise. I am indebted to Dr. James Ragan of the University of Southern California and especially indebted to Luna Carne-Ross and Lois de la Haba.

FIRST EDITION

Copy editor: Bruce Emmer
Indexer: Maro Riofrancos

Library of Congress Cataloging-in-Publication Data

Davis, Margaret L.
  Lovers, doctors, and the law.

  Includes index.
  1. Sexually transmitted diseases—Law and legislation—United States.
2. Liability (Law)—United States.   I. Scott, Robert (Robert S.)   II. Title.
KF3803.V3D38   1988   344.73'0436951   87-45607
ISBN 0-06-055111-9   347.304436951
ISBN 0-06-096236-4 (pbk.)

88 89 90 91 92 MPC 10 9 8 7 6 5 4 3 2 1

Contents

Introduction: Promises in the Dark

Promises in the dark. . . . Who hasn't made them or received them in moments of passion? But are they kept when the lights go on? Not only your relationship but very possibly your health—maybe even your life—depends on the answer to that question. And on it, also, depends your status in the eyes of the law.

Sexually transmitted disease (STD) outbreaks have reached epidemic proportions in our time. To curb the spread of these diseases we need all the weapons we can muster. Truthfulness in matters of medical history is one of them. The law is another. My interest in the legal aspects of sexually transmitted disease brought me to realize what hardships mere unthinking careless-ness could cause. The law, I feel, not only can compensate vic-tims for their suffering and their expenses but—even more im-portant as far as I am concerned—it can act as a deterrent. And that is my primary aim in writing this book.

What do I mean by trust, by promises between lovers? In the present context, I mean the pledges they make to be open and truthful with each other about their health. These promises are an expression of love, a proof of human decency and consider-ation, a necessary component of any real relationship. However, they are also considered binding in legal terms. In the eyes of the law, people who have sex with each other have a "fiduciary" relationship—that is, a relationship of *trust*. This is so not only in long-term serious commitments but even in the most casual one-night stand.

As for ethical and moral issues, we still mostly cling to the assumption that no decent person would knowingly and willfully harm another, and this is probably true. But those promises in the dark can be—and are—broken. Why? Because we harbor secrets and can find it hard to reveal them—because we do not know how to communicate.

One purpose of this book is to show you and your lover how to share your most intimate secrets, how to communicate with perfect frankness about your sexual and health history, and how to keep those promises made in the dark—or at any other time.

Failure to do so can be expensive. The court system imposes civil liability for promises that are untrue, misrepresented, or fraudulent. In addition, there are federal and state statutes that deal with the transmission of diseases, in some cases making such transmission a crime. Where morality is not enough to control a sexual partner's inclination to lie about a medical condition, the law affords its own type of protection. Your promise in the dark may have to stand up in the spotlight of courtroom proceedings.

This book examines in detail the legal risks inherent in transmitting STDs to others. It explains the basic legal concepts: What is the difference between negligence and intentional torts, for instance? What type of behavior makes you vulnerable to civil action? To criminal prosecution? What damages could you be liable for? It further discusses the legal impact of STDs on divorce, annulment, and child custody. It studies the effects of discrimination faced by STD sufferers in all areas of their lives (including the discrimination children face in school) and the legal paths of coping with them.

State by state, the book details the laws dealing with STDs. Who can be sued and why? Where is transmission a crime? When is it grounds for civil action? What are the statutes of limitation? Which states prohibit lawsuits between spouses or unmarried lovers?

The legal problems connected with the epidemic outbreaks of STDs, from syphilis to AIDS, are new—or at least the legal attitude toward them is new. That is why this whole area of law is at present in a state of flux. New legislation is being considered and passed on the federal and state levels. Court decisions in seminal cases are setting precedents. It is essential to seek the advice of an experienced attorney who will know the best and most appropriate way of presenting any case.

Our self-image and sexuality are bound up with how we feel about ourselves and our "significant others." Failure of trust is a denial of ourselves. That is why we need to feel that our partner cares enough to give honest promises. Therein lies the importance of promises in the dark: they are kept in the light of day.

1

Before Making a Promise

I only want what any other girl wants. Tall, dark, handsome and disease free.

—*New York City woman*

The most wanted commodity in today's marketplace is safe sex. But is there really such a thing? Whether you're married or single, gay or straight, old or young, making love isn't simple anymore. You're not just having sex with one partner. You're having sex with all the partners your lover has slept with for years past. You've got to assess the inherent risks of sleeping with a group of invisible lovers whom you don't even know. That is why, nowadays, any kind of sexual relationship, even the one-night stand, demands some sort of commitment for yourself and your partner.

Every sexual encounter presents unknown risks, and therefore you have to start out by asking yourself two crucial questions: (1) Do I really want to assume the responsibility for those risks? (2) Do I know my partner well enough to take his or her answers on trust? The answer to the first question can come only from you. For the second one, you'll need to know your lover.

AIDS inspires the most fear these days, but for the average

4

person the other STDs are without a doubt a more present danger. If you are sexually active, ycu are quite likely to find yourself confronted with the issue in your own life.

There will be 14 million new cases of STD infection this year, and 65 percent of these will occur among young people 25 or under. New evidence suggests that exposure to one or more STDs can result in suppression of the immune system, and infection has now been linked not only with an increased risk of getting AIDS but also with at least six different cancers.

The STD epidemic has forced us to rethink and restructure our love life. But while we can no longer give in to our sexual instincts without restraint, we don't have to swear off sex altogether. With the help of some old-fashioned notions—trust, morals, ethics—we can once more come to a point where promises between lovers are meaningful.

As an attorney I have seen the heartaches my clients and others have experienced as a result of false promises from a sexual partner. The lovers of these victims may not have intended to hurt anyone or transmit VD but they were careless, and that carelessness cost their partners a great deal.

One thing is certain: Lovers who have been infected through the misleading or false statements of their partners suffer deep-seated pain. They feel rage toward the partner who was at fault. And in some cases the anger extends to the medical profession and the opposite sex in general.

From researching cases for my clients and other lawyers, I can tell you firsthand how real and grievous these injuries are. In some instances, plaintiffs have faced serious medical complications and/or severe financial hardships. Some have lost their jobs through disability or discrimination, others have lost custody of their children.

Patients with easily curable STDs like gonorrhea or syphilis can suffer emotional and psychological complications, even after the illness has been successfully treated. But with diseases like incurable genital herpes or chronic condyloma (genital warts) the shame and anger are not so quick to dissipate. Doctors report that many patients experience stages similar to those mourning the death of a loved one: shock, emotional numbing, isolation and loneliness. Depression and impotency are not uncommon.

It can happen to anyone. A virus knows no morals nor class distinctions. Ordinary people, professionals, politicians, all have found themselves in the same difficult situation. In one leading case in California, a nurse contracted genital herpes from a physician who lied to her about his condition. A prominent banker has been sued by his wife for infecting her with venereal disease. Lawsuits have been filed between lawyers for negligent transmission.

Movie stars and other celebrities have confronted the issue in their private lives. In New York, 24-year-old Linda Feldman has sued singer Tony Bennett for $90 million claiming that he infected her with genital herpes. In Los Angeles, Marc Christian has filed suit seeking $24 million against the estate of Rock Hudson charging that Hudson deliberately lied to him about AIDS.

Misrepresentations that result in infection can be costly. For married couples, negligent transmission often ends in divorce. In a romantic partnership that is supposedly monogamous, the news that one partner has contracted an STD is explosive. Lovers who have caught incurable, recurrent genital herpes are particularly susceptible. "In a monogamous relationship," *Time* magazine stated, "the unsuspecting person who picks up herpes from a partner is hit with a double whammy: evidence of betrayal and a lifelong disease as a memento of the event."

Under the law, an individual is entitled to compensation for the physical and (in most states) emotional injuries that have resulted from the original illness. Increasingly, lovers are taking their plight to the courtroom, and, where appropriate, are recovering stiff dollar damages (typically $100,000 or more) from the sexual partners who, intentionally or negligently, infected them. Each case, however, has its individual aspects, state laws differ, and each jury weighs evidence in a different way.

Legal action is not always appropriate. Not everyone wants to open up his or her personal sex life to public scrutiny. Many would rather get on with their lives than consume themselves in a costly and humiliating court battle. Some cope more successfully than others. The decision to sue is profoundly personal.

My intention here is not to advocate lawsuits between lovers but to promote honesty. I simply want to inform all sex partners about the importance of promises made in the dark—for their own sakes, for the emotional and physical health of their lovers.

Later in this chapter, the Lover's Legal Checklist will show you a new way to exchange promises which can limit both legal liability and the risk of infection. It is the most desired dialogue between lovers before they engage in sexual intimacy. It may be appropriate in your personal situation, or it may not be necessary. But it's as good as a lawyer in your pocket as a tool to help you get through the maze of fear and insecurity surrounding the entire STD issue.

For those who have been lucky enough to escape infection, the Lover's Legal Checklist can prevent it from happening in the future. For those who already have encountered the issue—and for everyone, no matter what your personal situation or health history—knowledge of your legal rights is your best defense.

Getting Started

It is easy enough to approach the subject when your partner is as interested as you are in safe sex. But not everyone is. Some people feel that there is no need to be totally honest. If your partner is one of them, the decision is strictly up to you: How willing are you to take the risk, legal as well as medical?

You may agree that trust and communication are essential in a committed relationship, but hardly when it concerns something you know for a fact can't last. But because of the new risks associated with lovemaking—and now the important legal considerations as well—trust and communication are just as important in short-term sexual encounters as they are in long-term relationships.

Whether you're confronted with someone you feel you can

trust or someone you're not so sure about, the personal checklist that follows will help you put the situation in perspective. Ask yourself these questions before embarking on any sexual relationship:

1. What do I really want?
2. How sexually active do I need to be?
3. Do I have enough information to have sex that is free from legal liability and medical risk?
4. Am I ready to do this? Am I willing to commit myself to the possibilities or the responsibilities?
5. Can I make a genuine promise? A real promise without deception or a hidden agenda?
6. Can my partner make a genuine promise? Do I know this person well enough to believe in the truth of his or her answers?
7. What do I want out of this? What does he or she want? Is it a recipe for love or disaster?
8. Is my ability to judge impaired for any reason?
9. Will he or she keep the promise?
10. Will I?

"SO, WHAT DO I SAY?"

Male virgins are the "hottest new commodity on college campuses," according to a new study reported in *USA Today*. The reason? The fear of sexually transmitted diseases.

The survey, conducted by New York psychologist Srully Blotnick, reports that college women are more attracted to male virgins now than they were before. Ten years ago, Blotnick says, "very few women wanted their lovers to be bumbling, awkward and inexperienced. . . . Now women are chasing the more innocent male partner. The male virgin may not make the best lover," Blotnick said, "but usually he's eager to learn—and he's the safest."

Before you limit your choice to a partner who's never had sex before consider this alternative: Get to know your partner better. One good approach is a heart-to-heart talk before the moment of truth. But before you can be assured that the answers to your questions are honest you must really know the person you are talking to. Only by taking the time to do this can you be confident that your lover's assurances are true.

Open talk about your sexual history before starting an affair is difficult under any circumstances, and the less familiar you are with your prospective lover, the harder it is. Therefore, the first step is to let the relationship grow until you feel reasonably comfortable about revealing the most intimate details of your physical and sexual self. Then pick a time when both of you are relaxed and at ease. Don't blurt out a dozen legal questions just as you're tearing off your clothes or are about to fly off for a romantic weekend in the tropics.

Talk is part of your commitment. You both have the right to know everything before you're heavily involved. Just remember one thing: The right time is always *before* sex, not after!

Where should your heart-to-heart conversation take place? Any place is right as long as you can talk without interruption and at length. Forget a crowded party or a noisy disco. Give your partner time to react and respond in kind. It takes time to develop a meaningful dialogue. One woman, in a letter to *The Helper* (Herpes Resource Center, Fall 1985) advises that she found the kitchen especially conducive to such confidences. A good alternative, she says, is talking on a long walk. The worst place, according to her, is the bedroom.

The toughest part is getting started. Here are some possible opening lines:

- "I really like you. Would you be comfortable enough to tell me about your recent sex life?"
- "When two people get along as well as we do, I think we owe it to each other to be totally honest. That's why I'd like to share my own sex history with you and want you to do the same with me."
- "I want to make love tonight. But I need to know if you've had sex with anybody else since we last made love. . . ."
- "I think we're both responsible adults who want to do what's best for each other and for ourselves."

- "Before we make love, I'd like to tell you how I feel . . ."
- "I love you. Let's talk about real promises about our health."

Take it one step at a time. Show that you care, and that caring will repay you handsomely.

Breaking the News: How to Tell a Partner That You Have an STD

If you have a contagious medical condition, you can still have sex, and you can still make real promises. Having an STD should not be a threat or a bar to sustaining or developing a loving relationship. Imaginative lovers have always found ways to satisfy their physical desires in spite of temporary handicaps.

The big question is when and under what circumstances a medical condition should be disclosed. From a legal point of view, the best advice is to disclose *any relevant* history before a relationship is consummated. Even if you had a short bout with gonorrhea years ago, you are duty bound to tell a new partner. For incurable and recurrent infections such as genital herpes, a reminder of your medical condition is a must *every* time you engage in sexual intimacy.

How you and your partner handle other problems in your life will determine to a large extent how you will handle this one. It is no cause for alarm, nothing to be frightened about. But it has to be dealt with realistically. This book has all the information you need to act with confidence and knowledge. Talking everything over and clearing the air is the only way to tackle it.

The biggest obstacle to breaking the news is the fear of rejection. Remember these points:

You are not a virus.   A disease is only one very minor part of your biological makeup. It has nothing to do with you as a loving human being. Don't let a disease destroy your self-image as a sexual person.

It can happen to anyone.   A virus has nothing to do with social registry, money in your pocket, social habits, or intelligence. It doesn't make you dirty or less attractive. It is a health problem that should be treated like any other disease. You owe it to yourself and your loved ones to treat it responsibly and objectively.

Forget "all or none" thinking.   Telling the truth doesn't mean instant and permanent rejection. Sex isn't out. Only impulsive sex without a frank exchange of one's history is. During an infectious period, there are other ways for you and your partner to enjoy sexual intimacy. Erotic stimulation can be carried on safely outside the genital or other infected areas.

We don't call our sexuality into question when we restrain our sexual activity because of a cold or other illness. Why do so with a virus like herpes or an illness like chlamydia? A disease is not an emblem of impaired sexuality. It is a problem with a solution.

What if I get rejected?   The intimidating part of making a real promise is the fear of rejection. Remember that thousands of talented, intelligent, and attractive people get rejected every day. It is reasonable to expect that some individuals will relate to you, and others reject you for your unique personal characteristics: it is unlikely that anyone would base a judgment solely on a troublesome medical condition.

Some people believe their attractiveness and desirability have been damaged by disease. Do not let such a thought undermine your efforts to relate lovingly to others. If someone you're attracted to focuses on the disease to the exclusion of all else, set that person straight or walk away. It's that person's problem, not yours.

Sex is still in the game plan when people care and are informed. Focus on loving rather than being loved. This will help you overcome your vulnerability to rejection and facilitate communication.

Avoid doom and gloom.   Never preface your remarks with anything that remotely sounds like "I've got this terrible thing to tell you ..." or "Better sit down, something awful has happened..."

Avoid nightmare words. Attitude makes a big difference. While this is no joking matter, a light touch helps. Tell your partner, for instance, that you won't reveal your bank account, but you'll do better—you'll reveal your health secrets.

Make your conversation as comfortable as possible. Here are some possible suggestions to help you break the ice:

- "I'd like to share with you some of my sexual history. Last year I contracted..."
- "I've recently been tested for VD. I'm afraid I can't make any promises about my health until I get the results..."
- "I've had some problems in the past with genital warts. I don't think I've got them now, but just to be safe let's use a condom..."
- "I've got an appointment with a doctor at the health clinic. Why don't you come with me and we'll get checked out together?"

Tell the truth.   Stick with the facts. Otherwise it will come back to haunt you. You risk legal liability and endanger your credibility if you allow even one white lie to slip out.

Don't worry in advance.   It won't help. Instead, plan your talk ahead of time and rehearse it in front of the mirror if you feel you need to. Make a capsule outline.

Get help.   Use whatever resources you have at your disposal. If you have a medical condition, a knowledgeable friend or doctor can help you explain your situation better.

Don't be surprised if he or she has it too.   One out of every five sexually active adults has or has had a sexually transmitted disease. Your own frankness may elicit frankness from your partner as well, which can only help you both.

Be honest about actual symptoms.   If you've had gonorrhea or syphilis before, you will remember what it felt like just before an occurrence. With genital herpes or chlamydia the same rules apply. Always be honest with a partner about your symptoms. Diseases can be contagious during the prodrome—before an outbreak or before visible signs appear. See Table 1 for a brief description of STDs, their most common symptoms, and their treatments. Consult Appendix II for more detailed information.

Hats off to condoms but beware.   Condoms are always a good idea if you've had any STD, past or present, or if you're with a partner whose sexual history is unknown. But use of a condom will not necessarily prevent the risk of infection or legal liability.

If you are currently contagious with any STD, condoms may not be completely effective when symptoms are present.

If you are a woman with a disease, the condom only protects the area of a partner's skin that is covered by the condom. Other skin surfaces, such as thighs, scrotum, perineum, and buttocks can remain exposed either directly to sores or to infectious secretions.

If you are a male with a current infection, a condom can prevent transmission only if it completely covers the area of infection. Sores outside the penis would not be covered. A partner's skin could be exposed to infectious secretions. Also, extreme care would have to be taken to prevent getting infectious material from the sores on the outside of the condom when putting it on. Common problems such as accidental breakage, slipping, and improper use are also important considerations.

Talk it over with your partner. Abstain from genital sex when necessary. A condom is helpful, but it's no guarantee of safety, either medical or legal.

Table 1
A Brief Course in Sexually Transmitted Diseases

Description	Symptoms	Treatment

AIDS

Infection with human immunodeficiency virus (HIV). Attacks body's immune system and impairs ability to fight disease.	Fatigue, weakness, swollen glands, fever, sore throat, skin rash, night sweats, headache. Diarrhea and weight loss follow.	There is at present no known cure. Opportunistic infections are treated as they occur.

Chlamydia

Infection with *Chlamydia trachomatis* micro-organism. Can cause pelvic inflammatory disease, mucopurulent cervicitis, ectopic pregnancy, and sterility.	Genital discharge, spotting, vaginal itching and burning, fatigue, flulike symptoms, burning urination, pelvic pain, and low-grade fever. Often victims have no symptoms until there are complications.	Ampicillin and tetracycline in combination. Curable.

Genital Herpes

Infection with herpes simplex virus. Implicated in cervical cancer. Can lead to reproductive complications.	Painful anal and genital blisters and ulcers of skin and mucous membranes. Fever, muscle fatigue, headaches.	Zovirax (acyclovir) delays recurrence. CO_2 laser lessens frequency and severity of recurrence. Incurable.

Table 1 (continued)

Description	Symptoms	Treatment
Genital Warts Infection with human papilloma virus (HPV). Affects internal and external genitals, skin, and mucous membranes. Implicated in cervical and genital tract cancers.	Itching, small superficial anal/genital growths, body warts. Symptoms may be absent.	CO_2 laser is recommended treatment, with very low recurrence rate. Traditional superficial treatments are generally ineffective and painful. They can also be toxic. Curable.
Gonorrhea Infection with *Neisseria gonorrhoeae* bacterium. High risk of pelvic inflammation and sterility. May lead to arthritis.	Yellow genital discharge (pus), in both men and women. Painful urination in men. Pelvic pain in women. Women may be asymptomatic.	Ampicillin and tetracycline in combination. Curable.
Hepatitis B Infection with hepatitis B virus. May be major cause of liver cancer.	Nausea, vomiting, loss of appetite, profound fatigue, diarrhea, dark urine, light stools, yellowing of skin.	Inoculation with immune globulin immediately after exposure. Vaccination with Heptavax B. Incurable.
Syphilis Infection with spirochete of *Treponema pallidum*. Contagious, deadly disease whose damage is irreversible. Attacks all body tissues and organs. Silent and insidious.	Painless oral, genital, and rectal ulcers. Sore throat and/or rash.	Penicillin G and tetracycline. Regular follow-up blood test every 3 months for 2 years after treatment. Curable.

A Sample Case

The legal issues involved are deadly serious. It's not funny to think that somebody can tell a white lie that can hurt so much. But without some humor, the entire issue of safe sex becomes a difficult burden. Humor can be the release mechanism that opens up communication and gets the secrets out, and laughter is a universal medium for getting a point across even to a hostile audience. If you can reach somebody you care about through humor, it's worth a try.

But you also have to know when to get serious. If your partner doesn't seem interested, it's probably because he or she doesn't have enough information to recognize the risks. If your lover doesn't believe the issues are a personal concern, provide the facts.

If the facts don't do the trick, a fictional illustration might. The case of Dick and Jane provides a hypothetical example that illustrates some of the legal issues involved. (If your partner is still not concerned, you should think twice about the relationship.)

JANE V. DICK: A LAWSUIT AFTER ROMANCE

Dick and Jane grew up and fell in love. They were upwardly mobile kids who were serious about their careers. They both had good jobs and a good sex life. They were doing just fine until 1987, when a problem appeared on the scene: Dick came down with a case of genital herpes.

What the future holds for both of them will depend on how Dick handles the situation.

Scenario One

Dick develops a sore on his genitals and goes to the doctor. A physical exam and a culture indicate he has genital herpes. The doctor explains to him that herpes is infectious during the first signs of itching, tingling, and redness and remains so until the sore is completely healed. The doctor cautions Dick to abstain from contact in the infected area.

Later, Dick and Jane go to bed. He isn't sure how to approach the subject, so he doesn't tell her about his condition. He does practice prevention as the doctor prescribed: He abstains from sex when he thinks he is contagious, and thereafter he uses a condom.

By accident, Jane contracts herpes from Dick anyway. When she confronts him, Dick confesses that he didn't know how to tell her. Jane calls her doctor and makes an appointment with her attorney at the same time.

Dick's lawyer argues that Dick took reasonable care not to infect Jane. Jane's lawyer in turn claims that "reasonable care" under the circumstances was full disclosure and that Dick had a legal duty to warn Jane of his condition.

Who was right and who was wrong?

Dick had a *legal duty* to warn his girlfriend of his contagious medical condition, even if Jane didn't ask—and even if he used a condom. He needed to get the secret out and put it on the table so that Jane would be able to make an informed decision about taking the risk, instead of relying on implied false promises. Then they could have continued the intimate relationship, with appropriate safeguards and communication as equal partners.

Jane should have asked Dick if he had a medical condition that she should know about. She also needed to ask if he had slept with anybody else since they last had sex. She should have conducted her own quick undercover examination. Instead, Jane trusted Dick blindly and relied on a silent promise that turned out to be untrue. The court may hold that there was some contributory negligence on Jane's part, but that does not absolve Dick of his responsibility.

Scenario Two

Even after the first sore or repeated ones appear, Dick is unaware of his condition and does not go to his doctor. He never says anything to Jane and does not use a condom. Jane subsequently contracts genital herpes. Where does this leave Dick in the courtroom? Although he may have been honestly ignorant, that fact alone will not eliminate his legal liability. Because he did have sores, it can be argued that Dick should have known better.

Scenario Three

The story begins as in Scenario One, but Dick tells Jane everything. Knowing what she does, Jane still agrees to have sex. If she then contracts genital herpes, both lawyers feel that Dick would have a good defense.

In all three cases, the final decision is the court's. It will have to decide what a person exercising "reasonable care" would do in each one of these situations. Did Dick know about his condition? Did he disclose it fully? Or did he withhold information and attempt to prevent transmission? Was Jane fully informed about the potential consequences of sexual contact? Did she understand what she was being told? Did she really consent?

If the former lovers' stories differ, the jury as fact finder has to determine who is telling the truth. Can Dick convince the jury that he made full disclosure, that Jane knowingly agreed, and that events happened as he said they did? Or do the jurors believe Jane when she tells them that he said nothing?

If a jury finds Dick negligent, Jane might receive compensatory damages. Punitive damages could also be awarded if the jury finds not only that Dick was negligent but that the act of transmitting herpes involved an intentional, conscious disregard of Jane's rights and safety.

At any rate, Dick's and Jane's attorneys are busy preparing a case that should have been prevented by a genuine promise in the dark. As it is, the lovers have exchanged the bedroom for the courtroom.

The Legal Issues

The case of Dick and Jane illustrates some of the complex legal issues involved and their effect on the sexual activities of millions of men and women. A Washington *Post*/ABC poll has found that half of all young, unmarried Americans who consider themselves vulnerable to this type of situation are changing their sexual behavior.

The one-night stand has lost much of its popularity. The threat of a lawsuit after casual sex is now a reality, and the informal approach is being superseded by frank and specific questioning by both partners about disease and medical history. So much for romance.

Because of the staggering statistics—STDs are epidemic—everyone needs to be aware of the legal consequences of sexual activity. Persons who have STDs either knowingly or unknowingly and fail to warn prospective sexual partners are prime targets for litigation.

Legal actions are not, however, clear-cut. They depend on the particular facts involved in each case and the laws of the state in which the case is being tried. A defendant who intentionally or accidentally transmits VD can find himself confronted with civil and in some cases criminal court action.

Should you or your partner find yourself with an STD after sex, the legal consequences can range from financial expenses to a jail term. First of all, the injured party can bring a civil lawsuit for monetary damages. In addition, the state can instigate criminal proceedings. About half the states have laws that make the transmission of an infectious disease a crime. Depending on the statutes of the individual states, transmission of venereal disease can range from a misdemeanor all the way to a felony.

If shyness, inexperience, or indifference tends to make anyone reluctant to disclose intimate sexual and medical facts, there are sound legal reasons that should convince everyone to overcome such reluctance.

The different kinds of liability and their grounds are:

CIVIL LIABILITY

The Law of Torts

A person can be liable for damages if he or she is found to have committed a *tort*. A tort is a wrongful act or injury committed by one person against another.

Torts are governed by the laws of each particular state, and they can be of two types: intentional or negligent.

Intentional tort.   Here there is the intent to commit harm—the actual, conscious desire on the part of one person to infect the other. In this category, suit can be brought for the following reasons:

- Intentional transmission of disease
- Battery
- Intentional infliction of emotional distress
- Fraud (willful concealment)
- Misrepresentation (deceit)

Negligence.   This is behavior that falls below the legal standards defined to protect people from harm or the lack of due care that a reasonable person would be expected to exercise in given circumstances. To determine liability in negligence, the following facts will have to be established:

- The defendant knew or should have known that he or she had the disease.
- The defendant did not take reasonable precautions to avoid infecting the plaintiff.

Causation

For either intentional tort or negligence, the plaintiff must show *causation*—that is, the cause of the injury, without which this injury would not have been sustained. For this, the following need to be established:

- Can the specific source of infection be traced to the defendant?
- What facts can be demonstrated to prove the defendant alone is liable?

Damages

An award of damages can be either compensatory or punitive.

Compensatory damages. These are to compensate the injured party for loss of earnings, diminution of earning capacity, medical and other expenses, and pain and suffering.

Punitive damages. These can be awarded where the defendant's conduct is "sufficiently outrageous" to warrant punishment beyond the simple compensation of the victim for actual damages. Such punitive awards are often made in fraud cases, including willful and negligent exposure, where the defendant knew of the existence of the condition and willfully infected the plaintiff. The economic wealth of a defendant may be considered by the judge or jury if punitive damages are sought by a plaintiff.

CRIMINAL LIABILITY

Criminal liability covers prosecution by a state against a person who committed an act punishable by law. The transmission of a communicable disease, including a venereal disease, is considered such an act in more than half the states. The crime may be a felony, possibly carrying a five-year term of imprisonment, or it may be only a low-level misdemeanor, with penalties that can range from a $100 fine to six months' hard labor. Further aspects of the criminal law are discussed in Chapter Four. (And a state-by-state guide describing relevant health code statutes and penalties appears in Appendix III.)

Your first obligation to yourself is to be as certain as possible that your lover's assurances are true. The easiest way to do this is to make sure your partner is aware of the legal facts about tort law that I've just described. Human nature is such that even the most indifferent person will think twice before being put in legal jeopardy through false statements.

But how can you make sure that your partner is aware of these facts without bringing along a lawyer on your date? Here is a legal checklist that all lovers should go through before engaging in sex, especially with a new partner. It is a new way to exchange promises, and the very fact of making them with legal and medical knowledge means there's a good chance they will be kept.

A Lover's Legal Checklist

Before engaging in sexual intimacy, consider these points to avoid both legal liability and the risk of infection. These questions may seem tough to handle in a romantic setting, but they are necessary to an exchange of genuine promises. They are the heart of your commitment to a healthy, meaningful relationship for you and your sexual partner.

Adapt this checklist to your own particular needs. Whether you use all of it or part of it depends on you and your partner, your sexual history, and your personal concerns.

1. SHARE YOUR MEDICAL HISTORY

Exchange with your lover:

- When you've each last had a medical checkup.
- What, if anything, that checkup showed.
- Whether either of you has had any recent STD symptoms. (See Table 1, page 14.)
- Whether previous lovers exhibited any of these symptoms.
- If either of you has a medical condition, whether it has been treated and cured. If it is recurrent or chronic, when were dates of occurrences?
- Information about any blood transfusions received before 1985 (when effective blood screening for AIDS began).

Consider a joint visit to the doctor.

2. SHARE YOUR SEXUAL HISTORY

- Discuss your recent sex life.
- Is either of you bisexual?
- Were any partners in a high-risk group?

3. ACT WITH INTEGRITY

- Make your promises genuine. Get all the secrets out.
- Don't let passion cloud your better judgment. Make sure that any risk you take is full and informed—not under the influence of drugs or alcohol.
- Be practical: Suggest a condom or spermicide.
- Be careful: Exchange letters with your partner.
- Make a physical examination part of your foreplay.
- If you have an STD, make sure you have met your legal responsibility to your partner through full and complete disclosure. Your legal duty can be met with three simple words—for example, "I have herpes."
- Be trustworthy: Keep the information about your partner confidential.

4. TRUST YOUR FEELINGS

- Don't underestimate your inner voice. If you feel insecure about your partner, practice caution.

A Lawyer's Legal Checklist

If you should get an STD, you may need a lawyer. Here are some of the questions your attorney will want you to weigh before deciding whether you should and want to sue.

- History of relationship with the defendant
- Medical history of plaintiff and defendant
- Sexual history of plaintiff and defendant

- The actual injury:
    Date, time, and place
    Medical evidence
    Mental and physical condition of both partners
    Use of condoms or spermicide
- Plaintiff's efforts to question or examine the defendant
- Representations of the defendant
    Did plaintiff assume any risks?
    Were they full and informed?
- Defendant's reputation in the community
- Defendant's financial status
    Employment
    Homeowner's insurance
    Other assets
- Plaintiff's motive for legal action
    Revenge
    Compensation
- Plaintiff's willingness to submit to intense scrutiny of his or her private life.

Thoughtful use of the Lover's Legal Checklist will, I hope, make the Lawyer's Legal Checklist obsolete. When it comes to safe sex, selfishness is a virtue. Your partner should appreciate it as much as you do.

Lovers must ask questions *before* they engage in sexual intimacy. Use the Lover's Checklist as a resource for better communication. Don't be afraid to use it. It can preserve your good health and peace of mind.

2

Lovers and the Law

Love is like a roller coaster. You ride it, it makes you scream, but [on the roller coaster] you know you're safe the entire time. The thing about love is there's no seat belt . . . and the next thing you know, one of you is flying.

—Lynda Barry

In the time it takes you to read this sentence, a man or woman between the ages of 15 and 30 will get a sexually transmitted disease. No one intends to contract a contagious disease. But it happens. And it happens often. In this country alone, more than 38,000 people become infected for the first time with an STD each and every day.

More and more of these people want redress, and as they become aware of their legal rights, they are increasingly turning to the courts. Lovers who once would not have told their best friend they suffer from a venereal disease are sharing their sexual experiences with judge and jury.

WHAT ARE THE CHANCES THAT YOU MIGHT END UP IN COURT?

The chances are good that you'll end up in court if you're the giver or receiver of false promises or untrue statements or if the disease is negligently transmitted. *Time* magazine (June 8, 1987, p. 78) says: "Increasingly, outraged spouses and lovers . . . are suing their partners for infecting them."

Plaintiffs have demanded stiff compensatory and punitive damages, ranging from $100,000 to millions. In one sensationalized case a Kansas City socialite slapped her prominent husband, one of America's ten best-dressed men, with a $6 million lawsuit for infecting her with genital herpes. Her case received unprecedented media attention.

Sensational or not, such media coverage is useful. Fourteen million Americans will become infected with a sexually transmitted disease this year, and experts estimate that more than half are infected because of fraudulent misrepresentations by a sexual partner. A person who is aware of the legal liability of deceptive promises and its public consequences is more likely to inform a potential partner about the risk of infection.

A Stupid Mistake, but at What Cost?

Courtroom drama is not just for the stage! Men and women have suffered real injury because of false statements made by their sexual partners. A careless or unfeeling sexual transgression can result in years of unhappiness, discomfort, or worse, especially in cases involving incurable genital herpes or the life-threatening AIDS virus. Therefore, injured persons have every right, legally and morally, to sue their guilty partners. Victims are not only demanding—and sometimes collecting—substantial amounts of money, but they are also helping to clarify and even change the laws dealing with STDs. For instance, Nurse Kathleen K.'s suit against her doctor lover in California led to a historic ruling by the California court of appeals in 1984 that set a legal precedent for the nation and will have a profound impact on how cases are handled. (See Chapter Three for the full story.)

In Wyoming, attorney Gerald Spence helped pioneer STD litigation in 1979, when he won a verdict of $1.3 million for his client, a young college coed who suffered life-threatening complications from the negligent transmission of gonorrhea. (This case is also detailed in Chapter Three.)

Nor are the lawsuits restricted to partners. In the country's first third-party suit involving a married couple, a University of Louisville law professor sued a local lawyer for $250,000 for allegedly infecting the professor's wife with genital herpes. Professor Leonard R. Jaffee claimed that defendant Steven Wade Dillis fraudulently and willfully concealed the disease from Mrs. Jaffee, who later infected her husband. (The case illustrates the problems in third-party liability further explained in Chapter Five.)

Grounds for Redress

How can a victim of infection obtain redress for the physical, emotional, and psychological harm caused by the transmitter? The purpose of the law in torts is to afford compensation for injuries sustained by one person as a result of the conduct of another.

An injured plaintiff is allowed legal remedies for a punch in the nose or an automobile accident. The transmission of disease falls in the same class, whether the infection is spread intentionally or through negligence.

In 1894 an English court indicted a mother who carried her smallpox-infected child on a public road on the grounds that such exposure endangered the health and lives of the king's subjects. This rationale has been expanded by modern civil liability law to the general principle that a person who negligently exposes another to a contagious transmissible disease is liable in damages. In other words, courts place the burden on the infected individual *not* to transmit the disease to others.

Cases governing actions between sexual partners involving the transmission of venereal diseases have been on the books in the

United States since the early 1800s. The social stigma attached to such cases inhibited exposure, but some plaintiffs pursued their legal rights in the first half of this century despite public embarrassment and humiliation. As Americans have become less secretive about sex and more litigious, the number of legal actions has grown apace.

Until the outbreak of the genital herpes epidemic and the realization of its serious nature, this disease had not been among those brought to court. Since the late 1970s, however, it has spawned a growing number of lawsuits. Many of these cases have now been resolved, and the court decisions are affecting AIDS and all other STD litigation by establishing clear precedents as to when and why partners can start legal action. This type of litigation focuses on the issue of candor between partners *before* sex.

The Law

The basic rules of law are clear and simple: It is the legal duty of a person with an STD to warn others or to take measures to prevent infecting them. Failure to do so makes a person guilty of *tort* (a wrongful act, injury, or damage for which civil action can be brought) and allows plaintiffs who have been infected to be compensated for the injuries sustained. A plaintiff who is wrongfully infected can sue for negligence or for intentional tort, which includes battery and fraud.

The details are more complex, and they determine the course of action a plaintiff will choose, depending on the circumstances of the individual case.

INTENTIONAL VERSUS NEGLIGENT CONDUCT

The legal meaning of *intent* is straightforward. As Justice Oliver Wendell Holmes observed, even a dog knows the difference between being tripped over and being kicked. The difference between unintentional and intentional conduct is also the key distinction in two major divisions of legal liability—negligence and intentional torts. It is a basic concept in the way our laws are organized and enforced. One fundamental question an attorney will ask his client is, Was the defendant's conduct *intentional?* The answer to that question will be central in a decision to pursue legal action for intentional torts like battery or fraud or to pursue remedies in negligence.

The concept of *intent*, as described by legal scholar William Prosser, encompasses "not only . . . those consequences which are desired, but also . . . those which the actor believes are substantially certain to follow." For example, a defendant who pulls a chair out from under an unsuspecting plaintiff intends that the plaintiff will fall but may not want the plaintiff to break his leg. However, such injury is a direct consequence of the defendant's physical action aimed at the plaintiff. This would make it an *intentional* tort.

The *Restatement (Second) of Torts,* (a volume containing a restatement of the laws followed by most courts) provides another example: A throws a bomb into B's office for the purpose of killing B. A knows that C, B's stenographer, is in the office. A has no desire to injure C but knows that his act is substantially certain to do so. C is injured by the explosion. A is subject to liability to C for an intentional tort.

In contrast, look at the following example: On a curve in a narrow highway, A wants to pass B's car and recklessly speeds up. A has no desire to injure B, nor is he substantially certain that he will do so. However, as a result of A's reckless driving, his car crashes into B's, injuring B. A is liable to B for his reckless conduct but is not liable to B for any intentional tort. The only legal liability will lie in negligence.

The same distinction holds true in STD cases. It is accepted that an individual with venereal disease is "substantially certain" to pass it on to a sexual partner. The type of liability is decided by the following:

- The defendant is liable in *negligence* if he acted recklessly, below a reasonable standard of care but without any desire or intention to injure his sexual partner. This would be the case if the defendant *knew or should have known* of his disease but he failed to exercise the appropriate care.

- The defendant is liable in *battery, fraud, or intentional infliction of emotional distress* if he not only knew about his contagious medical condition but deliberately had sex anyway with the conscious intention or the substantial certainty of transmitting the disease to his partner.

The distinction between intentional torts and negligence has a dramatic impact on legal liability. There is a tendency to impose greater accountability on a defendant whose conduct was intentional or morally wrong. A defendant is subject to the least liability where his conduct was inadvertent or accidental. As far as compensation for a plaintiff is concerned, the determination of conduct as either intentional or negligent plays a significant role in the award of damages.

Negligence

The core of a claim in negligence is the requirement that a defendant knew or should have known he had a contagious disease prior to transmitting it to a sexual partner.

Negligence has been defined as conduct that falls below the standard of care expected from a reasonable person. Most people are familiar with the term *negligence* because it is commonly used by plaintiffs in a typical rear-end collision or a medical malpractice claim.

The traditional legal concept of negligence is flexible enough to fit modern contexts like STD litigation. As one attorney for an early herpes plaintiff commented, "If you're hit at a crosswalk, it makes no difference whether it's by a 1964 Chevy or a Buck Rogers antigravity machine. . . . The fact that it's a new vehicle doesn't mean you need a new theory."

The measuring stick used to judge whether a person's conduct was negligent is typically the "reasonable person under the circumstances" test. This is a broad phrase used to determine whether conduct was beneath the standard insisted on by society.

Four *elements* are necessary for action in negligence:

- A duty of care on the part of the defendant
- A breach of that duty
- Causation
- Actual loss or damages

The accidental or careless transmission of disease is actionable whenever the defendant failed to exercise a reasonable standard of care. Courts recognize the duty of sexual partners not to infect one another carelessly.

Such negligent conduct can include:

- Careless exposure to disease
- Careless failure to detect the disease by medical or self-examination
- Careless failure to discover an outbreak
- Careless failure to inform a partner
- Careless failure to prevent transmission (failure to abstain from skin contact in a contagious area, failure to use condoms)
- Any combination of the above

An infected person has a duty to avoid this kind of behavior. If a defendant's conduct falls below this standard and causes the transmission of an infection to another person, the injured victim has a right to recover in negligence.

The tort of negligence was perfectly illustrated recently in *Star* magazine (April 4, 1987) when an anonymous man seeking advice wrote:

> I'm carrying around a load of guilt that would sink a ship. For a year now I've known I have herpes, but I didn't have a recurrence until a week ago. When I think of all the women I've slept with in the past year, my conscience goes crazy. I never told them I had an incurable disease. Now that I've come to

my senses, I don't have anybody to talk to. Are there places
you can go to share feelings like mine?

All those women he slept with would have a perfect case against
him, and the man would certainly need a lawyer.

THE DEFENDANT'S DUTY OF CARE

Most people recognize a *moral* and *ethical* duty to warn a potential sex partner about a contagious condition. Whether a person
owes a *legal* duty to a sexual partner is the essential question
in these negligence actions. Establishing the legal duty of care
depends on the circumstances in each case. Courts typically apply a balancing test. Some of the principal considerations in such
cases have been these:

- The foreseeability of harm
- The burden of disclosure on the defendant (balancing
  the cost to the defendant to do what he should have
  done against the potential risk to the plaintiff)
- Public policy considerations of preventing transmission
- Moral blame of defendant's conduct

The burden of disclosure on a defendant is considered relatively slight compared to the risk of infection to his partner, and
on balance a duty will be found to exist. The public health concerns of controlling infectious diseases and the moral blame attributable to defendants who avoid the problem can easily tip the
balance in favor of the plaintiff.

The *foreseeability of harm* is of primary importance in establishing the duty to disclose. The position there is that the defendant should have foreseen the risk of transmitting the disease if
he knew or should have known that he had it.

Courts have taken as "knowledge" the existence of the infection itself, a visit to the doctor, or the application of prescription
medicine. In a disease like genital herpes, obvious symptoms plus
consultation with a physician enable a plaintiff to establish that
the defendant knew or should have known of the disease. Any
circumstantial evidence, such as a previous diagnosis or an ad-

mission about the disease to someone else, could be used to show that the defendant owed the plaintiff a duty of full disclosure.

Clinical manifestations of disease take on different appearances. A person experiencing a first episode of genital herpes, for example, may honestly believe he is suffering from a simple skin irritation or other minor ailment. The court will determine whether the defendant failed to act *reasonably* in determining the true nature of his illness, failed to exercise proper judgment in consulting a doctor, or failed to take other appropriate measures. If so, he can be held liable even if he did not have actual knowledge of the disease.

BREACH OF DUTY

Once a plaintiff has shown that the defendant knew or should have known he had the disease and should have foreseen the risk to the plaintiff, the defendant's duty toward the plaintiff has been shown. The breach of that duty is established by the defendant's failure to warn a partner or to take preventive measures.

Why is there an obligation of disclosure by a defendant and no duty of the uninfected partner to inquire? It is the defendant who exposes his partner to the risk of contracting a disease through harmful contact. Applying a simple balancing test, it is easy to see that the defendant should bear the legal burden of full disclosure. Courts impose complete disclosure on the defendant with knowledge of a foreseeable risk but as a general rule will not impose a legal obligation on an uninfected partner to inquire.

A person who is contagious but abstains from any sexual activity has *no* duty to disclose his medical condition. By definition, the sufferer has taken appropriate safeguards to prevent negligent transmission.

A *breach of duty* can be found where a defendant did any of the following:

- Failed to take reasonable care in determining the existence of infection
- Failed to disclose a relevant medical condition

- Failed to warn
- Failed to take precautionary measures

Since reasonableness is the primary issue in negligence, defendants may try to defend themselves on the basis of a "heat of passion" theory. According to it, rationality is affected by powerful, uncontrollable sexual urges. Therefore, no duty should be imposed. The analogy is to cases involving drunk drivers or persons high on drugs. Courts have rejected this defense and maintain liability for the consequences of a defendant's behavior, whether intoxicated or sexually aroused.

A breach of duty is found where a defendant behaves in such a way that he creates an unreasonable risk of harm to his partner.

Statutory Enactments and Negligence Per Se

In states that make it a crime to expose another person to the risk of infection, the very fact that a law has been violated by the defendant establishes a breach of duty. Lawyers call this doctrine *negligence per se*. In these situations the extent of the legal duty of care is measured by the existing statutes rather than by the mythical "reasonable person."

State legislatures pass laws that impose obligations to act in a certain manner under certain circumstances. Where such a law exists, and is broken, negligence is presumed, and a defendant's claim that he exercised due care will not generally permit him to escape liability.

(A full discussion of statutory enactments appears in the state-by-state legal guide in Appendix III.)

CAUSATION

Causation is a difficult concept to grasp, and law students spend months analyzing its meaning in different contexts.

After establishing that a defendant breached his duty of care, the plaintiff must next prove causation. Lawyers break this concept into two distinct categories, causation in fact and proximate or legal causation.

Causation in Fact

This is determined by the jury, which has to consider the facts presented by both sides and decide whether the defendant's conduct actually caused the plaintiff's injury.

A plaintiff must show, through testimony, physical evidence, and medical reports, that the defendant's negligence was the actual cause of the plaintiff's injury.

Obviously, a person who practices sexual monogamy will have no difficulty in establishing the exact source of infection. A plaintiff with multiple sexual partners will. However, tests are being sought that will facilitate identification. For instance, there is already such a test for herpes: experts can now establish the source of infection despite multiple partners with a "DNA fingerprint" test. Through a technique known as restrictive endonuclease analysis it is possible to "fingerprint" a virus and trace it back to its suspected source. In the future defendants may have greater difficulty in claiming that a plaintiff cannot establish causation.

To prove actual causation a plaintiff must convince the court that based on the evidence presented, it is more likely than not that the conduct of the defendant was the cause of the resulting harm.

(The intricacies involved in proving causation in STD litigation are described in Chapter Five.)

Proximate or Legal Causation

Proximate or legal causation relies on the laws applicable to the facts under consideration by the jury and therefore the question of the defendant's liability. It is part of the instructions a judge gives the jury before it retires to consider a verdict.

Legal causation focuses on who should be held accountable for the harm suffered by the plaintiff. If a defendant had a duty to the plaintiff, if it was breached, and if the defendant's conduct was the actual cause of the plaintiff's harm, under the law the defendant will be liable. The liability question in a situation between two lovers is fixed on finding the breach of duty.

Proximate causation, however, may be a more complex issue

where more than two parties are involved. If Dick transmits a disease to Jane, who in turn infects John, Dick's act would be the *actual* cause of John's injury. Whether Dick's act was the *proximate or legal cause* of John's injury is another question. As a practical matter, questions of causation are treated as questions of fact and are almost routinely submitted to the jury. (Proximate causation that limits extended legal liability through a chain of sexual partners is also discussed in Chapter Five.)

After actual and legal causation have been established, the plaintiff must prove one more element for a prima facie case of negligence.

ACTUAL LOSS OR DAMAGE

The plaintiff must prove he has suffered some type of injury. Physical harm suffered by plaintiffs from the various venereal diseases will differ in duration and degree. Damages for curable STDs like syphilis, gonorrhea, and chlamydia—when no complications occur—may be less substantial, but it is clear that a plaintiff has been harmed once the disease is transmitted.

Persons with incurable genital herpes or chronic condyloma acuminata (genital warts) that are persistent and resistant to treatment can suffer psychological as well as physical harm. Individuals who have been infected with the deadly AIDS virus suffer unbearable injury.

Chapter Six gives more information on damages awarded as a result of a plaintiff's negligence.

SAMPLE CASE

Dick has been having sexual intercourse with Jane off and on for the past six months. During their relationship he slept with one other woman; Jane remained monogamous. Dick notices a strange-colored discharge and burning on urination. He carefully examines himself for any lesions or other symptoms and finds none.

Dick continues his intimate relationship with Jane. He doesn't bother to tell her about his unusual symptoms. He plans at some point to see a doctor.

Seven to ten days later Jane develops the first signs of gonorrhea. When Jane visits her gynecologist, she learns she has contracted a venereal disease from Dick.

Dick has been negligent in failing to have his condition diagnosed and disclose it to his sexual partner. Dick failed to see a
doctor and failed to prevent transmission of a contagious disease.
He carelessly exposed Jane to harm. Jane can pursue an action in
negligence.

AIDS: A SPECIAL CASE?

Although transmission of the AIDS virus by hypodermic needle
is not strictly within the scope of this book, it is included here
because further transmission of the virus can happen through
sexual intercourse, and such transmission usually falls under the
heading of negligence.

A damage action in negligence can accrue where a transmitter
with AIDS shares a contaminated hypodermic needle. The plaintiff would, of course, have to show that his injury (infection with
the AIDS virus) was caused by the defendant's breach of duty to
the plaintiff.

The standard of care or duty owed the plaintiff by a person
sharing needles may be established. It is clearly *foreseeable* to a
prudent person that sharing hypodermic needles may result in
the transmission of the virus and that transmission of the virus
may result in the development of AIDS.

The burden on the defendant of guarding against the transmission of AIDS through IV needles is not great; the infected person
might take care not to share needles with others or take care
to sterilize reused needles. This is not much of a burden when
balanced against the potential injury to the other. The safety of
the plaintiff and the great social benefit in preventing the spread
of AIDS are enough to expect the defendant to exercise a reasonable standard of care.

A person who allows another to share unsterile needles (especially given the general understanding that the disease is spread

through contaminated needles) fails to meet the standard of conduct for a reasonable person and, if causation can be proved, may be guilty of negligence.

Defenses

A defense of *contributory negligence* (conduct on part of the plaintiff, sufficiently connected to the harm, that falls below the standard of care to which he is required to conform for his own protection) may be a valid defense to a charge of negligence in this context.

Given the widespread understanding that contaminated hypodermic needles can spread the disease, a person who shares unsterilized needles departs from the standard of care of a reasonable person. As a result, a plaintiff who alleges that the defendant caused the transmission of AIDS quite likely will be barred from recovering damages, or at least may have any damage award reduced, as a consequence of his own negligence.

In an assumption-of-the-risk defense, the defendant must prove that the plaintiff voluntarily incurred a *known* risk that resulted in his injury and thus assumed that risk. Unless the plaintiff's drug companion warned him that he had the disease and that sharing the needle could later lead to infection with the deadly AIDS virus, the plaintiff could not know that he risked contracting the disease through the use of a hypodermic needle.

In absence of full disclosure and full understanding by the plaintiff of the nature of the risk involved, a defendant will not be able to assert this defense to shield himself from liability.

LEGAL CAPSULE

- CAUSE OF ACTION: Negligence
- DEFINITION: Conduct that involves a foreseeable risk of harm and falls below a reasonable standard of care
- POSSIBLE DEFENSES: Due care, assumption of the risk, contributory negligence, failure to establish proximate causation
- DAMAGES: Compensatory; in extraordinary circumstances, punitive damages may be awarded

---

Battery

When a defendant knows that he has a contagious venereal disease and knows that the probability of transmitting it is great, sexual activities that result in infection can constitute the intentional tort of battery.

In the law books a battery is defined as an unconsented, unprivileged touching. Actions in battery can result from something as significant as a punch in the nose or as innocuous as knocking off another person's hat.

An unwanted kiss can be grounds for battery. In Minnesota, plaintiff Neil Johnson testified that a kiss he received was "offensive." The unwanted smooch won him $375,000 when, after six hours of deliberation, jurors ruled that a judge committed battery by kissing his male court reporter.

The touchstone of a successful claim in battery is an unpermitted contact that is offensive to the sensibilities of the average person. Obviously, if one person has sexual contact with another against his or her will, a battery has occurred. But even if both partners consent to the sexual relations a battery may be committed if consent is obtained by misrepresentation.

Three elements are necessary to prove a civil battery in cases of STD:

- Intent (the deliberate intent to transfer the disease or the intent to cause the contact that causes the disease, such as sexual relations)
- Contact (an actual touching)
- Offensive contact (a touching that offends a reasonable sense of personal dignity)

Consent is a defense to an allegation of battery, and a defendant may argue that the plaintiff agreed to the sexual intercourse, which constituted the touching. But where the plaintiff did *not* have knowledge of a partner's infectious condition, it does not follow that in consenting to have sex the plaintiff also consented to being infected with a sexually transmitted disease. A woman's consent to sexual intercourse is invalidated by her partner's fraudulent concealment of the risk of infection.

The touching between lovers engaged in intimate sexual activities must be seen as two separate and distinct touchings:

- Sexual touching (within the plaintiff's consent)
- Contamination with an infectious disease (outside the plaintiff's consent)

Under this analysis, a plaintiff's consent to engage in sex does *not* constitute consent to the second touching, the transmission of disease. The defendant has failed to obtain effective consent and is therefore liable for infecting the uninformed partner. The tort committed is called a battery.

Many states adopt the *Restatement (Second) of Torts* (compilation of laws) approach:

- If A consents to sexual intercourse with B, who is aware that A does not know B has a venereal disease, B is liable to A for battery.
- A's consent is ineffective because it was the result of A's mistaken belief that B was free of venereal disease.
- If B misrepresents that he is free from venereal disease, despite his knowledge of infection, and that misrepresentation induces A to engage in sex, B is also subject to liability for battery.

A person who intentionally or knowingly induces another person to use a hypodermic needle contaminated with HIV (human immunodeficiency virus, the virus that causes AIDS) commits a battery. This too is considered an intentional, harmful, and unprivileged contact with another. The element of intent may be inferred from the recklessness of allowing another human being to share a needle that the user knows could be contaminated with the AIDS virus.

Battery is also illustrated in another AIDS-related context: A woman sued American Airlines for $12 million because one of the airline's employees, a carrier of AIDS, bit her. The complaint charged not only battery but intentional infliction of mental distress as well.

SAMPLE CASE

Dick and Jane have been dating for several weeks. Dick is aware that he is experiencing an outbreak of genital herpes and is also aware that Jane doesn't know this. In spite of that, Dick asks Jane if she wants to make love. Jane says yes. Jane and Dick engage in intimate relations. Soon thereafter, Jane contracts genital herpes. Jane would never have consented to sexual intercourse with Dick had she known of his contagious condition. Dick's touching was unpermitted, and Jane has grounds for an action in battery. This would have been equally true if Jane had asked Dick if he had an STD and he said no.

Because it is an intentional tort, Jane can seek punitive damages (designed to inhibit this kind of behavior) as well as compensatory damages (provided to compensate Jane for her injury).

LEGAL CAPSULE

- CAUSE OF ACTION: Battery
- DEFINITION: Intentional, unpermitted touching; touching without consent
- POSSIBLE DEFENSES: No knowledge of disease, consent by plaintiff (consent to sexual relations vitiated by misrepresentation of contagious condition)
- DAMAGES: Compensatory and punitive

Fraud, Deceit, and Misrepresentation

A lover who justifiably relies on the false promise of a sexual partner who claims to be free of infection and is not can seek action in fraud in addition to battery. At the heart of this legal concept is the question, Did the transmission of a contagious disease involve concealment or misrepresentation of material facts where there was a duty to disclose those facts?

There are five elements of fraudulent misrepresentation:

- A false representation made by the defendant
- Knowledge or belief by the defendant that the representation is false
- Intention to induce the plaintiff to rely on misrepresentation
- Justifiable reliance by the plaintiff on the promise
- Damage to the plaintiff resulting from this reliance

In an action for fraud, the plaintiff must show that the defendant actually knew of his condition and deliberately *withheld* the information to induce the plaintiff's consent to have sex or *lied* to the plaintiff about his sexual history and the plaintiff agreed to engage in sexual relations based on that false assurance.

The key points are that the defendant *actually knew* of his condition and that he made the misrepresentations with the *intent* of inducing the plaintiff into bed.

If no active misrepresentations were made by a defendant, does silence constitute grounds for fraud? The answer is yes, if keeping quiet was an active concealment of a relevant medical condition where there was a duty to disclose it.

There is a "fiduciary" (trust) duty in intimate sexual relationships. Lovers are duty-bound to act with the utmost care and confidence vis-à-vis each other because they share a trust and intimacy that elevates their relationship from that of friendship or mere acquaintance to something greater. It should bring about a heightened sense of confidentiality requiring the disclosure of important facts. The risk of contagious disease demands disclosure to a sexual partner, even in a short-lived romance.

In addition, silence can constitute deceit when the true facts are peculiarly within the knowledge of one party. In these cases the infected partner has exclusive knowledge of his condition. Failure to disclose it when appropriate is deceit and proper grounds for fraud.

The difficulty in pursuing a fraud action is proving the requisite elements of knowledge and inducement. If a plaintiff cannot prove that a defendant had *actual knowledge* of the disease, only that he *should* have known, a plaintiff should sue in negligence.

The question of *materiality* in each fraud case is determined by a jury. Courts typically find that a false promise or failure to disclose a contagious infection is an essential or *material* misrepresentation. Judges and juries find it difficult to believe that plaintiffs would voluntarily subject themselves to unnecessary risks.

A plaintiff's own negligence in relying on the defendant's misrepresentation is not a valid defense to fraud, because the defendant must intend to deceive his partner. Along the same line of reasoning, a plaintiff's contributory negligence (for example, seeing a sore on the defendant and not asking about it) is never a defense to intentional torts. If, however, a defendant can prove that a plaintiff had no reason to trust him, the plaintiff may be found to have assumed the risk.

In STD litigation, fraud is a primary cause of action. In many of these cases, plaintiffs directly asked partners if they had a contagious medical condition. In most instances, defendants simply lied.

One joke circulating on college campuses sums up the concept of fraud. "The three most popular lies are 'The check is in the mail,' 'I'm getting a divorce,' and 'It's only a cold sore.'" Dating rituals have changed, and it is no longer unusual for a partner to ask direct questions about medical history. That makes keeping quiet or lying about an important medical condition definitely grounds for an action in fraudulent misrepresentation.

If a court decides that punitive damages are also appropriate, a jury may consider a defendant's wealth in assessing a punitive award.

SAMPLE CASE

Dick and Jane meet at a school dance. There is a full moon, and the couple decide to take a walk. Soon they are kissing, and Dick suggests that they return to his dorm room.

The couple begin to make love. Jane is considering how to ask

Dick if he has anything she should know about. She is relieved when Dick whispers, "Oh, by the way, I do not have venereal disease." Based on his tender assurance, Jane makes love with Dick, confident that what he has told her is true.

Unfortunately, Dick's promise in the dark was false. Dick had been diagnosed as having syphilis by the university clinic two weeks earlier. Dick had been taking antibiotics, but he knew that he was still contagious.

Jane would never have had sex with Dick without his assurance that he was disease-free. She relied on a material misrepresentation of fact. Dick is accountable for fraud in a legal action by Jane.

LEGAL CAPSULE

CAUSE OF ACTION: Fraud
DEFINITION: Concealment or misrepresentation of a material fact that induces a plaintiff's reliance
POSSIBLE DEFENSES: Assumption of risk (plaintiff's reliance was not justified), no intent, no knowledge by defendant
DAMAGES: Compensatory and punitive

Intentional Infliction of Emotional Distress

The type of behavior that leads to liability for the intentional infliction of emotional distress is conduct that "exceeds the bounds tolerated by society" and is "extreme and outrageous."

Thirty-eight states recognize this legal action. The *Restatement (Second) of Torts* states that "one who by extreme and outrageous conduct intentionally or recklessly causes severe emotional distress to another is subject to liability for such emotional distress, and if bodily harm to the other results from it, for such bodily harm."

It strains the imagination to think that anybody would deliberately expose another person to a sexually transmitted disease.

But cases on record suggest that this type of behavior does occur. In Jackson, Mississippi, a homosexual transvestite with AIDS had been quarantined by authorities after he admitted he had deliberately exposed hundreds of men to the virus as a prostitute. A woman in Los Angeles claimed that she had infected 75 men in three years. A Pennsylvania man boasted he had deliberately infected 20 women.

Stories of people who have infected dozens of sexual partners are not uncommon. The desire to infect someone else may be based on an irrational form of "revenge" against the original transmitter that translates into vengeance on other sexual partners. One sufferer quoted in *Time* described a desire to "pass [the disease] on to everyone for vengeance until everyone had it and it became normal." Interestingly, the only person affected by these confessions was the transvestite prostitute, who was placed in police custody in Mississippi. The others continued to find and use victims.

Some courts have found the deliberate transmission of disease even to one partner sufficiently "extreme and outrageous" to warrant recovery from the transmitter for the intentional infliction of emotional distress that would clearly and certainly follow such an action.

There are two principal elements:

- Outrageous conduct
- Intentionally or recklessly causing severe emotional distress

This course of action is typical in STD litigation, especially in lawsuits involving genital herpes. Volumes of popular and medical literature outline the traumatic emotional impact of an incurable venereal disease such as genital herpes, which can damage an individual's self-image and sexuality. Such damage is well established. Deliberately exposing another person to the AIDS virus is also clearly grounds for intentional infliction of emotional distress.

Because the tort is intentional, punitive damages are available in addition to compensatory damages for physical and emotional harm.

SAMPLE CASE

Jane contracted genital herpes from her former boyfriend, Mike. Jane reacted to the infection with shock. She began a frantic search for a cure. After reading about the disease and speaking with her doctor, Jane understood that the disease was incurable and recurrent and as a result developed a sense of isolation and loneliness.

Jane sought psychological counseling at the local clinic. She experienced severe depression and believed that companionship and sexual gratification would never again be possible. As her concerns grew in intensity, anger became Jane's predominant emotion and eventually reached extreme proportions.

When Jane met Dick at a school football game, Jane was anti-sexual, angry, and hostile. Dick invited her out for drinks. He later made sexual advances, and Jane reacted by deliberately sleeping with him when she knew she was suffering an outbreak. Jane intentionally infected Dick because she wanted somebody else to suffer the way she did. Jane was fully aware that Dick would feel the same emotional trauma that she experienced because of the disease, but she slept with him anyway.

Dick can proceed in an action for intentional infliction of emotional distress against Jane.

LEGAL CAPSULE

CAUSE OF ACTION: Intentional infliction of emotional distress
DEFINITION: Outrageous conduct resulting in physical and emotional harm
POSSIBLE DEFENSES: No intent
DAMAGES: Compensatory and punitive

Actions in negligence, battery, and fraud are the legal remedies available to the injured plaintiff in STD litigation. Infection with a disease is as much a violation of bodily integrity as a punch in the nose. Real promises between lovers before sex, common sense, and the fear of legal trouble for lovers who lie about a contagious medical condition can prevent a bitter and public legal confrontation later.

As plaintiffs become more aware of their legal rights and sexual activities become less secretive, more lawsuits will be filed. A resulting legal epidemic of tort actions may in turn reduce the STD epidemic by encouraging honesty in sexual relationships.

3

Spouses and Lovers

Tort Liability in Marriage

Gretchen Stuber, a housewife in Bern, Switzerland, filed for divorce against her husband, a wealthy 36-year-old banker, and charged him with attempted murder. She also sued him for $10 million, claiming he knowingly exposed her to the AIDS virus.

Karl Stuber developed AIDS after a blood transfusion when he underwent heart bypass surgery in New York in 1981. He recovered from the operation and returned to Switzerland but was later notified by his doctor that he might have been exposed to the AIDS virus through contaminated blood.

A blood test in 1983 confirmed the presence of the virus, but Mrs. Stuber's lawyers claimed that Stuber withheld this information from his wife while continuing to engage in sexual relations with her.

"Karl Stuber might just as well have put a bullet into a revolver, spun the chamber, taken aim at his wife, and pulled the trigger," stated Hugo Vogt, Mrs. Stuber's attorney. "He chose to play Russian roulette with her life, and now he is going to pay."

When asked how the plaintiff ultimately learned of her husband's condition, lawyers conceded that Mrs. Stuber learned the truth after hiring private detectives to follow her husband on a business trip in 1986. She discovered that her husband was receiving treatment for AIDS at a Paris clinic. Mrs. Stuber moved out of the family home and filed for divorce.

Gretchen Stuber, 35, shows no trace of the virus in her bloodstream, but doctors caution that she could develop a full-blown case of the disease within seven years after exposure.

"For the crime of loving her husband," Mrs. Stuber's attorney stated, [Mr. Stuber] sentenced [his wife] to die."

Attorneys for Karl Stuber admitted their client is under treatment at a Paris clinic but refused to say whether the defendant is dying of the disease. "Whether my client is suffering from AIDS or a simple head cold, that's a confidential matter between him and his doctor."

Gretchen Stuber claimed that she "lives in terror" because her husband failed to disclose his "deadly secret." Lawyers anticipate an emotional and unprecedented trial.

DO YOU KNOW THE ANSWERS?

The Stuber case is apparently the first lawsuit anywhere between a heterosexual married couple involving the fraudulent misrepresentation and willful nondisclosure of the AIDS virus. It raises important questions about charges leveled between married partners concerning any STD:

- Can a wife charge her husband with attempted murder?
- Can spouses sue one another for assault and battery? Negligence? Fraud?
- Does a couple have to be separated or divorced before legal action is permitted between spouses?
- If a spouse is successful in legal action against his or her marriage partner, can the winning spouse collect proceeds from the partner's insurance policy?
- How are such insurance proceeds distributed at divorce?
- Is infection with an STD grounds for annulment of a marriage?

- Can venereal disease be used to demonstrate "cruel and inhuman treatment"?
- Can it be used to show adultery?
- Can infection with an STD influence the distribution of marital assets?
- Can one spouse testify against another in a court of law?

INTERSPOUSAL IMMUNITY

Until recently, husbands relied on the doctrine lawyers call *interspousal immunity* to protect themselves from being sued for tort liability by their wives. Interspousal immunity was the result of the common law holding that upon marriage, the legal existence of the wife was incorporated into her husband's and the two were thereafter considered "one person in law." Spouses suing each other would in effect be suing themselves.

As a result, a wife could not sue her husband for assault and battery if he beat her or for negligence if he failed to exercise a reasonable standard of care. Likewise, a husband could not instigate legal action against his wife.

The underlying concept was the public policy perception that permitting lawsuits between spouses would "destroy the peace and harmony of the home" and the "sacred relation[ship] of man and wife." Although courts recognized that infection of a spouse was an intentional tort, they followed this common-law notion in decisions involving STD litigation. In 1898 the Michigan supreme court refused to permit recovery for a wife whose husband infected her with syphilis, which was then incurable and a serious infliction. To permit the plaintiff recovery, the court stated, would "open the door to lawsuits between [married couples] for every real and fancied wrong." In case after case courts prohibited legal compensation for wives who had been injured by their husbands.

Although the law has changed considerably in the majority of states, there are still states in this country where wives are prohibited from engaging in legal actions against their husbands.

The concept of interspousal immunity began to erode in the mid-nineteenth century, when the states started enacting "married women's property" acts. The first to pass such an act was Mississippi, in 1839. In the succeeding half-century, every state in the Union adopted some form of this act. Under it, for the first time, women were given a separate legal identity of their own and gained the right to engage and control their own property, to work outside the home without their husband's permission, to retain the earnings of such employment, and to enter into contracts. They even gained the right to start legal actions or have legal actions brought against them. All these rights, however, concerned a woman's property. These new statutes also allowed a woman to bring action against her husband when her property interests were involved: She could sue him for fraud or trespass or to recover for conversion (the wrongful appropriation of property) or for negligent harm to her property. The husband, in turn, had similar rights to sue his wife for torts committed by her against his property.

But the married women's property acts were held *not* to destroy spousal immunity for personal torts, and during the remainder of the nineteenth century and most of the twentieth century courts refused to permit recovery against one spouse by another for either intentional torts (like battery, assault, intentional infliction of emotional distress, and fraud) or negligence.

One exception occurred in 1920, when a North Carolina court was moved by the plight of Lacy Crowell, a young bride who had unwittingly been infected with a painful case of syphilis only weeks after her wedding day. In that case the court construed the state's married women's property act as permitting a wife to maintain legal action against her husband for the intentional transmission of venereal disease. The court stated:

> Whether a man laid open his wife's head with a bludgeon, put out her eyes, broke her arm, or poisoned her body, he is no longer exempt from liability to her on the ground that he vowed at the altar to "love, cherish, and protect" her. We have progressed that far in civilization and justice. Never again will

"the sun go back ten degrees on the dial of Ahaz." (Isaiah
38:8)

The court reasoned that a brutal assault and battery had been
committed on young Mrs. Crowell by her husband and that infecting her with a "foul and loathsome venereal disease" caused
her serious bodily injury. The court awarded her a substantial
judgment of $10,000.

But the judge in the Crowell case was ahead of his times. It
wasn't until fairly recently that the concept of interspousal immunity was seriously questioned as arguments for upholding immunity became less imperative. By 1970 roughly a dozen courts had
rejected the principle of immunity between spouses. During the
next decade many dozens of other cases followed this lead, and
today spousal lawsuits for personal injury are permitted in a majority of the states, at least under some circumstances.

This leaves a respectable minority of ten states that still follow
the old rule and provide for absolute or near-absolute immunity
between spouses in personal injury tort claims. However, the
trend against such immunity continues, and it may be assumed
that more and more states will do away with it, in whole or in
part.

Although we are making progress in the general area of interspousal immunity, the archaic doctrine is very much alive and
well in another context—spousal rape. In about half the states a
husband is still legally incapable of raping his wife, although
some states permit legal action under certain circumstances (e.g.,
husband and wife are living apart or are legally separated). In
only eight states can a wife bring legal action against her husband
for rape with no strings attached.

The eight states that have fully rejected the marital rape exemption are:

Florida	New Jersey
Kansas	New York
Massachusetts	Oregon
Nebraska	Wisconsin

The rationale of exemption is based on the common-law perception that a wife's consent to a husband's demands of sexual

intercourse during marriage is irrevocable. In some two dozen jurisdictions, a husband cannot, with certain exceptions, face civil or criminal liability for rape—in spite of the fact that according to D. Russell, author of *Rape in Marriage,* at least 14 percent of all married women in the United States are raped by their husbands.

An article in the 1986 *Harvard Law Review,* "To Have and To Hold: The Marital Rape Exemption and the Fourteenth Amendment," makes the important point that "the marital rape exemption serves as both a manifestation of and vehicle for the continued subordination of women in society." The article also states, "a husband's violent sexual possession of his wife against her will is such a point of power. And the law's sanctioning of this exercise of power transforms this power into truth. Therefore, when men say, 'a husband cannot rape his wife,' they speak the truth."

This doctrine is purported to protect the sacred nature of the marital relationship. But surprisingly, ten states have recently expanded the marital rape exemption to cover even "unmarried cohabitators" and/or "voluntary social companions." This means that if Mary and John are living together without being married, Mary cannot institute legal action against John if he forces her to engage in sexual relations against her will in the following states:

Alabama	(1977)	Kentucky	(1985)
Connecticut	(1985)	Maine	(1985)
Delaware	(1979)	Montana	(1985)
Hawaii	(1984)	Pennsylvania	(1985)
Iowa	(1979)	West Virginia	(1984)

Legal exemption from the crime of rape during marriage is still on the books, but significant legal trends spell the end of the "irrevocable consent" doctrine in this or any other marital context. It is common sense, if not common law, that a spouse, just like any other injured party, should be able to institute legal actions for injuries suffered, including negligent or deliberate infection.

A handful of states still maintain full interspousal tort immunity. In these jurisdictions a woman cannot sue her husband or a husband his wife for the intentional or negligent transmission of disease under any circumstances:

Delaware	Hawaii	Montana
District of Columbia	Louisiana	Missouri
Florida	Mississippi	Wyoming
Georgia		

In courts that still acknowledge the rule, there is little a plaintiff can do to overcome it short of moving out of the jurisdiction. In order to preserve their right to instigate legal action, some spouses do in fact move to a state that doesn't follow the immunity rule.

Joanne N. St. Clair, the gutsy wife seeking $6 million against her husband for the infection of genital herpes, found her court action dismissed because of a Missouri law upholding interspousal immunity. Not to be thwarted, Mrs. St. Clair changed her residence to California, where the rule does not apply. Her action is now pending in California courts.

Some jurisdictions have found the rule unjustified and have created a hybrid of the concept. These states have kept part of the doctrine alive by abrogating it with respect to intentional torts but upholding it for negligent torts. In these states a wife *can* sue her husband for intentional tort (assault, battery, intentional infliction of emotional distress, and fraud) but *cannot* engage in legal action on the grounds of mere negligence.

In support of their decisions upholding the bar against negligence actions between spouses, these courts claim that the immunity is necessary to prevent fraud. One judge in Utah noted that the temptation to collusion exists where there is insurance and is increased where the adversaries are husband and wife. The natural reaction to defend a claim of negligence, the judge reasoned, would be supplanted by the covert hope of "mutual benefit." Many courts have agreed.

Five states have abolished the immunity rule for intentional torts but have retained it for actions based on negligence:

Illinois	Ohio	Texas
Kansas	Oregon	

Therefore, in courts in these states, if a spouse acted negligently but without intent to do harm, a plaintiff spouse might be out of luck and unable to pursue compensation for injuries.

Fortunately, the majority of jurisdictions have completely invalidated the interspousal immunity doctrine, but not until recently. Even the progressive state of California didn't get its act together on this rule until the early 1960s. Historically, California followed the common-law rule and refused to allow tort actions between husband and wife. In 1962 the California supreme court, in the landmark case *Klein* v. *Klein,* abandoned the rule. In states like California, plaintiff spouses can sue for intentional tort or negligence, and their claims will not be prohibited based solely on the marriage relationship.

Thirty states have fully invalidated the interspousal immunity rule:

Alabama	Iowa	New Mexico	Tennessee
Alaska	Kentucky	New York	Utah
Arkansas	Maine	North Carolina	Virginia
California	Maryland	North Dakota	Washington
Colorado	Michigan	Oklahoma	West Virginia
Connecticut	Minnesota	Pennsylvania	Wisconsin
Idaho	Nebraska	South Carolina	
Indiana	New Hampshire	South Dakota	

These states have generally taken the position of the *Restatement (Second) of Torts* that a husband or wife "is not immune from tort liability to the other *solely* by the reason of the marital relationship." STD cases where a defendant has deliberately infected a spouse present the perfect fact pattern to evoke the court's sympathy and incline it to go along with the *Restatement* position and permit suits between spouses.

Wives have been successful in tort actions against their husbands in states where the immunity doctrine is no longer good law. Plaintiffs in these actions have been awarded compensatory and sometimes punitive damages for the negligent or intentional infection with venereal disease by their husbands.

- A 68-year-old woman in Ottumwa, Iowa, won a default judgment of $50,000 from her ex-husband based on intentional infection with genital herpes. Compensatory damages were based on evidence of physical injury, embarrassment, and humiliation.

- In one case, a sympathetic jury awarded $40,000 to a woman who claimed her estranged husband gave her venereal disease during an attempted reconciliation.
- In April 1986 the supreme court of Missouri ruled that the long-standing doctrine of interspousal immunity did not bar a negligence action against a husband for the transmission of genital herpes.
- In December 1986 the New York supreme court ruled that a woman who had been married for 31 years could seek compensatory and punitive damages from her husband for the wrongful transmission of disease.

Many actions between spouses, especially in states where spousal immunity is accepted, are still pending. The issue the courts are deciding is whether interspousal immunity is still valid as applied to STDs. Lawmakers may find that the immunity doctrine has outgrown its usefulness. The justifications for its continued acceptance based on common-law rules of the oneness of husband and wife are no longer applicable. As STD litigation throughout the country receives more widespread attention and more plaintiffs exercise their legal rights, the spousal immunity doctrine may see its last days in the states that still follow the rule.

ANNULMENT

Courts are hesitant to grant an annulment after consummation of a marriage for anything less than physical impairment, an undisclosed prior marriage, a blood relationship (incest), underage consent, or fraud that goes to the very core of the marital relationship. Conversely, lies about wealth, personal habits, social status, chastity, and false vows of love have all been determined by U.S. courts not to be sufficient grounds for annulment.

Express misrepresentations made by a spouse can be sufficient to support an annulment, but they are dependent on the facts of each case. For example, a husband's failure to disclose that he had previously been married and fathered a child has been found insufficient legal grounds on which to base an annulment. A wife's misrepresentation that she was younger than her husband is insufficient premarital fraud on which to grant an annulment. But a husband's concealment of heroin addiction is a fraud that affects the essentials of a marriage and is thus valid grounds to annul the marital contract. So is a lie by either spouse about the existence of an STD.

In addition to express statements, some prenuptial representations are implied. These include the capacity and desire to engage in sexual intercourse and the lack of venereal disease. The passive concealment of such conditions can constitute valid grounds for annulment as well.

Is the Existence of Venereal Disease Grounds for Annulment?

Historically, it has been in most jurisdictions. In one early case on the issue in 1901, a New Jersey court found that the statement made by a man to his prospective bride that he was not afflicted with syphilis was a fraudulent misrepresentation that was crucial to her agreement to the marriage. The misrepresentation was therefore a valid ground on which an annulment could be obtained.

It is still valid law today. The purpose of marriage in the traditional view is procreation. The infection of venereal disease frustrates that purpose and goes to the very core of the marital relationship.

Whereas not telling a prospective spouse about being infected with an STD or lying about it is grounds for annulling the marriage contract in most states, continued sexual relations and cohabitation with a spouse after having been informed of the infectious condition are generally deemed a waiver of the right to annulment.

DIVORCE

A sexually transmitted disease given by one spouse to another is pertinent in the following issues concerning a divorce:

- As proof of adultery
- As constituting cruelty
- As evidence in divorce proceeding
- As a factor in division of marital assets

After a 31-year marriage, Jane Maharam filed for divorce on the grounds of adultery and cruel and inhuman treatment. In seeking a fair distribution of the marital property, Mrs. Maharam asked for compensatory and punitive damages of $2.5 million because her husband fraudulently or negligently infected her with incurable genital herpes. The New York supreme court upheld Mrs. Maharam's right to sue, ruling that marital partners have a legal duty to tell each other if they have a venereal disease.

A spouse's infection with venereal disease can have profound implications in divorce proceedings where it is used to demonstrate adultery or ill treatment. In some states the very transmission of a sexual disease to a spouse is considered "extreme cruelty" and grounds for divorce. To establish cruelty, the guilty spouse must have known of the infectious condition prior to transmission.

Other states need additional proof of domestic unhappiness and will not grant a divorce based solely on the contraction of disease. In these states, if other acts of cruelty are charged and if the disease undermines a spouse's physical health or peace of mind, courts find the STD an additional justification for divorce.

Charges of adultery (including promiscuity with prostitutes) are often made by spouses seeking a bigger division of marital property, and the contraction of a venereal disease can be used to suggest such illicit conduct. When testimony is introduced that a defendant willingly infected his spouse, it can weigh heavily in favor of the victim.

In Dallas a woman won a jury verdict of $375,000 on divorce and personal injury claims based on the transmission of *Chla-*

mydia trachomatis by her husband. The plaintiff, Mrs. Stafford, fully recovered from the disease, but her reproductive system was permanently damaged. The ruling was overturned by an appeals court because under Texas's long-standing spousal immunity doctrine a wife could not sue her husband. But in February 1987 the Texas supreme court gave the plaintiff new hope of collecting the jury award by challenging the validity of the immunity concept and sending the case back to court for review.

Mrs. Stafford used the evidence of her husband's extramarital affair and the subsequent infection of venereal disease to demonstrate fault and claim a larger portion of the couple's community property assets.

Many attorneys feel that wives should not be permitted to "pick and choose" a method, including the presentation of damaging evidence regarding the transmission of disease, for collecting in a divorce. But even in community property states that follow the "no fault" concept, such evidence is taken into account by the court in distribution of marital assets.

In states where grounds for divorce must be established, proof that a spouse has developed a sexually transmitted disease can demonstrate adultery. Infection to a plaintiff spouse can be evidence of "cruel and inhuman treatment." A court is more willing to award a wife a hefty settlement where the husband has engaged in extramarital conduct that has resulted in the spread of disease.

The issue is cropping up in dissolution proceedings around the nation. In one Florida divorce case a wife accused her husband of infecting her with genital herpes and asked the court to order him to pay all her future health and medical costs related to the disease. The court complied. The husband's lawyer has asked the Florida supreme court to review the case as a "question of great public importance."

False accusations by one spouse that the other had venereal disease can weigh in favor of the innocent spouse. In at least a dozen cases, spouses who have been falsely accused have been successful in demonstrating "mental suffering" as a result of the untrue charges and have benefited financially in divorce proceedings.

Vows recited between husbands and wives to "love and cherish" should not be broken through the reckless or willful transmission of disease. If it occurs, it may be proper grounds for dissolution of the marriage. It can also affect the court-ordered division of marital property.

IMPACT ON FAMILY LAW

Ronnie and Debra Bailey were divorced in 1979, and custody of their two minor children was awarded to the children's mother. One year later Mr. Bailey filed a petition to get his children back, alleging that Mrs. Bailey had contracted genital herpes and that the mother's disease "virtually mandated a change in custody."

In a unanimous decision, the Arkansas court of appeals ruled that a woman should not lose custody of her children because she had contracted a venereal disease. Judge Tom Glaze of Little Rock stated that "the mere fact of possible infection primarily transmitted by sexual activities did not have much significance as far as the children are concerned." Mrs. Bailey was awarded permanent custody.

The issue of venereal disease has been used by spouses involved in child custody litigation to change a custody ruling based on the premise that an ex-spouse who develops an STD is an unfit parent.

Some courts feel that sexual indiscretions do support a change in custody, and evidence of a spouse's infection is weighed against the parent with custody.

In Alabama a mother lost custody of her two children, aged 8 and 6, on the presentation of evidence that she entertained men overnight in the bedroom of the family home and had contracted genital herpes. Richard Sparks petitioned the court to obtain custody of his two minor children, Justin and Jody, and alleged that the mother's venereal disease was a serious medical virus that was contagious and a danger to the children.

On review, the court found additional evidence to support the determination that the best interest of the children was served by a change in custody and awarded care of the children to the father. The venereal disease seems to have had a role in that outcome.

Depending on all the facts and circumstances involved in each case, a court can support a change of guardianship based on the infection of an STD if other evidence corroborates parental unfitness or sexual indiscretions potentially harmful to the children.

In some cases, however, decisions are made solely on the basis of a disease. For instance, a judge in Indianapolis terminated a divorced father's visitation rights because he carries the AIDS virus, although he does not have the disease. The judge found that his condition "is a danger to the minor child's well-being."

In another case, a father in Pennsylvania was unsuccessful in winning custody of his daughter despite evidence that the mother admitted to seven different sexual contacts, mostly in automobiles, and the contraction of gonorrhea. The court found that the father had had sexual intercourse with a former wife and engaged in two additional acts of unchastity before filing for the change in custody. The judge commented that the "double standard is history and . . . he and she are two cats in a bag," obviously feeling that the father's behavior was no better than his ex-wife's. The presence of gonorrhea in itself was insufficient to warrant a change in custody in light of all the facts.

Progressive jurisdictions require more than the mere contraction of a disease to reverse custody decisions. Courts are willing to find, where the evidence presents itself, fitness in parents who were unlucky and contracted an STD. In cases where good parenting skills are demonstrated through evidence and testimony, many courts are sending a message that parents who happen to have VD have the same rights to custody and visitation as other parents.

Tort Liability for Casual Sexual Partners

Celebrated Wyoming attorney Gerald Spence won $1.3 million in a jury verdict for a young female college student who had been infected with gonorrhea through the gross negligence of her sexual partner.

Margaret Housen was living, working, and going to college part time in Washington, D.C. She was introduced to the defendant, "Pony" St. Angier Duke, by her brother. On the same night, following dinner and drinking, Margaret had sex with the defendant in the front seat of his pickup truck.

Four days later, after Pony's sudden and convincing statements about love and marriage, the plaintiff began a trip by truck from New York to Denver, "engaging on and off in sexual intercourse with defendant along the way." Two weeks later Pony broke off the affair and informed Margaret for the first time that he had gonorrhea and that now "she probably had it too."

Margaret later developed serious complications from the disease. Doctors conducted major exploratory surgery when the antibiotic treatment for gonorrhea proved ineffective and Margaret's pain became severe and constant. Her physician found that scar tissue adhesions had formed within her lower abdomen, and he was forced to cut the adhesions surgically to relieve his patient's pain. In court Margaret's physician testified that new adhesions would form again and continue in a cyclical manner for the rest of her life. Margaret's ability to bear children was also permanently in jeopardy.

The trial court sympathized with the plaintiff and awarded $300,000 in compensatory damages designed to cover hospital expenses, doctors' fees, lost wages, future medical expenses, and pain and suffering. The jury found that Pony Duke breached his legal duty of care to Margaret by failing to disclose that he was infected with gonorrhea and as a result was guilty of gross negligence. It awarded Margaret an additional $1 million in punitive damages by verdict. The dramatic punitive award was intended to punish the defendant and discourage similar conduct.

On appeal, the supreme court of Wyoming reversed the trial court ruling on the basis of an expired statute of limitations. The court ruled that except for the expired statute, the plaintiff had a valid cause of action. It stated that Margaret's claim was within proper principles of tort law and that one who negligently exposes another to an infectious or contagious disease can be held liable in damages.

The case of *Duke* v. *Housen* is a classic example of tort liability based on negligence between casual sexual partners. Pony and Margaret were never married; in fact, their sexual relationship was consummated on the night they met. Despite the brevity of the affair, Pony nonetheless had a duty to tell his partner that he had gonorrhea. The fact that the plaintiff and defendant were merely sex partners does not abrogate Pony's responsibility to act within a reasonable standard of care.

Margaret's giant punitive-damage award was a clear legal victory, but it was overturned on a legal technicality. Margaret was aware of her injury, but she didn't develop serious complications until later and consequently brought suit only after the statute of limitations had expired. Despite the technicality, in place was the clear ruling that even casual sexual partners can be legally accountable for negligence.

Because of the recent epidemic of genital herpes, many unmarried sexual partners have instituted legal action based on the intentional transmission of the disease.

One such case that has attracted a lot of attention is the one involving singer Tony Bennett. Linda Feldman, who filed a $90 million suit against the singer, claims he infected her with herpes during their eight-month affair. When she discovered the infection, Feldman says in a *Time* magazine article (June 8, 1987, p. 78), Bennett told her, "I've had it for years. You get used to it. It's God's way of giving your sex life a rest." Bennett denies that he has the disease and has filed a $100 million countersuit.

The landmark case of Kathleen K. set a precedent for the nation and in the near future should be included in every law student's tort textbook. *Kathleen K.* v. *Robert B.* was brought by a nurse who met a Los Angeles physician at a retreat in northern California, and engaged in a love affair with him.

Kathleen said she asked the defendant specifically if he had ever contracted genital herpes and that he told her he had not. According to Kathleen he later admitted that he had contracted the disease some years earlier. On Easter Sunday, Kathleen developed large and painful lesions. She claimed that when she asked her lover, a medical doctor, about the sores, he remarked that it was really "nothing" to be upset about.

Kathleen soon filed suit and charged Dr. Robert Bolander with battery, intentional infliction of emotional distress, negligence, and fraud. In trial briefs prepared by her attorneys, Kathleen alleged that the defendant, "by deliberately having sexual intercourse with plaintiff at a time that he knew he was a ... carrier of herpes, acted outrageously and ... exceeded the bounds of human decency," thereby causing "physical injury and severe emotional distress."

Kathleen's case was dismissed by a lower court for failure to state a cause of action—that is, she failed to state facts in her complaint that would give her the right to seek judicial relief—and judgment was entered in favor of defendant Robert Bolander. Two years later the district court of appeals reversed the decision. The defendant then filed a petition with the California supreme court, claiming that the suit was an unjustified and unwarranted intrusion upon his privacy. The petition was denied. The district court said in its ruling:

> The key word here is *unwarranted*. The right to privacy is not absolute. It is subordinate to the state's fundamental right to promote public health, welfare and safety. The disease is serious and thus far incurable. The interest of this state [is] in the prevention and control of contagious and dangerous diseases. The woman is not complaining that the man made her step aside from the paths of virtue. This is an action for damages based upon severe injury to her body.

Five years after the case was originally filed, and following bitter and sometimes heated confrontations between lawyers for the two parties, Kathleen settled out of court in 1987 for an undisclosed sum against the physician who infected her with genital herpes.

The appellate decision gave new hope to people who suffer from the disease for recovering from those who infected them through negligent, fraudulent, or intentional conduct. For Kathleen, the lawsuit was about truth between sexual partners.

"Someone was dishonest," she said, "and it profoundly and destructively affected my life." Kathleen's legal struggle, the first of its kind, set a legal precedent for the nation.

ILLEGALITY

Susan Liptrot received national attention when she appeared on the daytime talk show *Donahue* with attorney Terri-Ann Miller to talk about her case.

The plaintiff, a 24-year-old stamp cataloger from Sarasota, Florida, accepted an invitation from Richard Basini to mix business with pleasure on a trip to New York for the National Stamp Show in 1980. Susan claimed she contracted genital herpes from Basini during a "one-night stand."

According to Susan, Basini said nothing to her about the disease. Susan noticed suspicious sores on the defendant after having intercourse. When she inquired, Basini reportedly replied that "his doctor did not know what the sore was, but that it was not contagious." Two days later, Susan was in great pain. A physician diagnosed the symptoms as herpes simplex II. The doctor told her to advise her sexual partner.

Liptrot phoned Basini, whose reaction, she said, was, "Oh, I'm sorry." According to Susan, when she saw Basini at a stamp show some time later, Basini asked her not to tell anyone about "our problem." Nor did he offer to help her, she claims, either personally or with medical and other expenses. Finally, Susan became enraged and filed suit. "I want him to realize the gravity of what he's done to me," she said. The plaintiff instituted charges against Basini, seeking more than $5,000 in compensatory and $100,000 in punitive damages for the fraudulent concealment of his herpes infection.

In addition to the physical discomfort, Susan claimed she suffered from the fear of rejection. She believed no one would want to marry her because she had the disease. "The guys really run," she said.

Attorney Terri-Ann Miller supported her client all the way.

"Maybe some people will think twice before taking the risk of infecting another person with herpes. If Susan can save one person from enduring the agony she's been through, then win or lose, the suit will be a success."

Can Susan Win?

Liptrot and Basini were not married. They were one-time sex partners. Unlike the Kathleen K. case in California, Susan's claim is based in Florida. Fornication between unmarried persons is illegal in Florida. Partners who engage in sexual intercourse outside marriage are guilty of fornication under Florida's statutory laws.

Sex between casual partners is also illegal in at least 15 other states, although these laws are hardly ever enforced. In these jurisdictions, however, a defendant in a tort action for the spread of disease can defend himself on the basis of a legal doctrine lawyers call "illegality." The idea is that since the plaintiff was engaged in an illegal act (sexual intercourse while unmarried) with the defendant at the time of her injury, she has no right to institute legal action. The principle behind the rule is that "the law will not permit a person to take advantage of or acquire a right of action from his own unlawful act or wrong."

A good example is the 1931 case of *Martin* v. *Morris,* in which the plaintiff sued a doctor who had negligently injured her in the performance of an illegal abortion. The plaintiff was denied recovery because the injury occurred during an operation that was "illegal and immoral." Whether this law will be applied in cases like Susan's is not clear. However, as we shall see, it is likely that the illegality defense would not work here.

IS THE DEFENSE APPLICABLE IN STD LITIGATION?

In states where fornication between casual partners is illegal, is a plaintiff permanently barred from relief?

Historically, the answer was yes. In an English case a woman who was paid for sexual services over a period of four years became pregnant and had a child. Both the woman and her child were found to be infected with syphilis. Plaintiff sued her paramour for assault, claiming that her consent was procured by the defendant's fraudulent concealment of his syphilitic condition. The High Court dismissed the complaint because it was based on an immoral act, and "courts of justice no more exist to provide a remedy for the consequences of immoral or illegal acts and contracts than to aid or enforce those acts or contracts themselves."

A court also took a harsh view of a woman who believed she was legally married and therefore her case might have evoked a more sympathetic reaction. Court testimony revealed that the plaintiff was not in fact legally divorced from her first husband and that her second marriage was therefore invalid. When she sued the man she thought to be her husband for infecting her with gonorrhea, the court refused, ruling that their relationship was "illegal" and the consequences of her injury were "her own illegal act." The court found no underlying principle on which to grant recovery.

Fortunately, strong arguments can be presented against defenses based on illegality. First, a good argument can be made that fornication laws are unconstitutional and archaic. The Supreme Court has yet to rule definitively on the issue of whether a government may constitutionally regulate private sexual activity. But many lower courts have overruled state laws regulating sexual activity between consenting adults.

Even in a conservative state like Georgia, where fornication laws have always been on the books, a 1985 court of appeals ruling permitted a male partner to sue his female paramour for the negligent infection of genital herpes. The court ruled on the issue specifically, stating that a person could recover in tort for injuries sustained even from his own *criminal* conduct. To rule otherwise, the court stated, would be against the public policy of the state of Georgia.

More and more courts are willing to invalidate laws that discriminate against unmarried persons and invade the privacy of adults engaged in consensual sexual activity. But even if fornication laws are found unconstitutional, a defendant can still argue that plaintiffs like Susan Liptrot should not be allowed to win damages from an illegal act. That argument is not good, however, because victims like Liptrot are not "profiting" from an illegal or immoral activity but are being compensated for physical injury they suffered as a result of tortious conduct.

One of the strongest arguments against a defense of illegality is the idea that the plaintiff-victim is not *in pari delicto,* "at equal fault," with the defendant. Even in states where fornication is a crime and a plaintiff's casual sex is illegal, the plaintiff's conduct is far less culpable than that of a partner who knowingly transmits a disease.

In a transmission case the victim is less guilty than the transmitter. Courts recognize that the illegality defense will not prohibit a plaintiff's recovery where a plaintiff "stands in a lesser degree" of guilt than a defendant. Some judges have ruled that while a victim's conduct may be deemed blameworthy under a state statute, a plaintiff's violation of the law is no defense if the defendant "acted wantonly or maliciously."

In the Liptrot case, Richard Basini presumably knew he had genital herpes and he acted maliciously when he failed to tell a new sexual partner. Liptrot should be able to pursue her cause of action. To deny recovery on the grounds of old statutes that may even be unconstitutional shelters the wrongdoer and makes little sense.

Plaintiffs like Susan Liptrot and Kathleen K. are entitled to their day in court, and their right to sue should not be denied on the basis of fornication laws that are outdated and rarely enforced. Defendants should not be able to rely on a defense of illegality to shield themselves from moral and legal responsibility.

In the Liptrot case, it appears that defendant Richard Basini quickly agreed on damages and settled out of court as Susan's trial date neared.

4

Criminal Liability

Everyone takes for granted that there are laws against murder, theft, and other such crimes. Few people, however, know that in many states it is also a crime to infect a sexual partner with an STD.

Such laws exist not only in the United States but also in many other countries around the world. In the Soviet Union, for instance, it is a violation of the criminal code knowingly to infect someone with a venereal disease, a crime punishable by three years in prison.

The communication of venereal disease to a partner can come under two categories of crime, misdemeanor or felony. The distinction between the two is the penalty.

- A *misdemeanor* is punishable by less than one year in the county jail and/or dollar fine or probation for a period determined by the court.
- A *felony* is punishable by a sentence exceeding one year in a state prison; the sentence is established by the state guidelines covering the specific criminal offense.

Generally, the court has discretion to sentence a convicted defendant. Where the sentence is specifically mandated by state law, a judge must follow this mandate and punish a convicted criminal accordingly.

In Alabama the offense is a misdemeanor, and a guilty defendant can be sentenced to six months of hard labor. In Tennessee and Wyoming courts can impose a $500 fine. In Oklahoma the communication of venereal disease is a felony, punishable by five years in prison. One man there was sentenced to five years in the state penitentiary after infecting his 16-year-old girlfriend with gonorrhea. (See Table 2, page 72 for individual state provisions.)

It is true that these laws are not often enforced. This was brought out recently when New York's governor, Mario Cuomo, startled observers by suggesting that the legislature consider making the transmission of AIDS a crime. In New York, as in a number of other states, AIDS is not classified as a sexually transmitted disease. Cuomo pointed out that such AIDS legislation would parallel an existing law that made infecting someone with an STD a criminal offense, although nobody could remember when anyone had been prosecuted for that crime. At present this is true in most states: Such prosecution is the exception rather than the rule. However, this may very well change in the near future as one way of combating the STD epidemic, and AIDS in particular.

Some lawmakers are already considering legislation that will make the spreading of AIDS a criminal offense. For instance, several such proposals in California include stiff criminal sanctions for people who infect others with the disease. And not only Governor Cuomo of New York but other influential individuals have voiced interest in such proposals. Paul Gann, a leader in California politics, who contracted the disease from a blood transfusion during heart surgery in 1982, even went so far as to say that people who knowingly pass on the disease should be tried for murder. Gann, who is dying from an AIDS-related illness, stated that knowingly infecting others was tantamount to pronouncing their death sentences.

Other states are also taking action. *ABC Evening News* reported, on June 22, 1987, that at least six states have passed legislation or have legislation pending that would require "prosecution and/or quarantine for anyone ... who fails to warn sex partners" that he or she has AIDS. New Jersey has the most extreme bills, requiring jail sentences of up to five years and a $7500 fine.

The states include Colorado, Connecticut, Florida, Idaho, Indiana, and Minnesota. Florida and Idaho have already made it a crime knowingly to expose another to AIDS. Colorado and Indiana have passed laws that permit persons with AIDS to be isolated. One Jackson, Mississippi, male prostitute, James McIntyre, was required by state order to warn all sex partners about his infection. A state authority issued the order after learning that McIntyre had expressed the desire knowingly to infect others with the disease. In Miami a convicted female prostitute with AIDS was held in isolation for over a month while authorities argued about what to do with her.

The Colorado State Health Department has adopted a regulation requiring the reporting of individuals whose antibody tests are positive. A physician has to report the infection, and sexual partners will be traced. Civil libertarians are concerned that the reporting and tracing of sexual partners raises serious constitutional issues. Some analysts fear that maintaining lists of seropositive persons is not sufficiently justified by a compelling state interest and may involve serious invasions of privacy and ill-conceived efforts to quarantine.

Critics feel that such actions will drive AIDS carriers underground and make the problems worse. They claim that the lure to legal protection will do more harm than good.

AIDS infections clearly pose a most extreme danger and for this and other reasons have spawned the most controversy. But even less serious STDs are cause for concern, and the possibility of even a short jail term is an obvious deterrent to people who might be inclined to mislead a partner about medical history.

The policy underlying these laws is public health. Virtually every state has statutory provisions on the books dealing with some aspect of the health hazards presented by STDs.

A state's ability to enact legislation to promote public health is based on its "police power"—a right granted states by the U.S. Constitution to enact legislation to safeguard the health, welfare, and safety of its citizens, including laws to prevent the spread of infectious diseases: for instance, requiring physicians to report such diseases, quarantine, and criminal sanctions ranging from fines to jail terms.

Table 2

Is it Illegal to Infect Someone with Venereal Disease?

State	Type of Crime	Provisions of Law
Alabama	Misdemeanor	Person afflicted with VD who shall transmit, assume the risk of transmitting, or do any act likely to transmit VD to another is guilty of a misdemeanor. Fine not less than $10 or more than $100. At the discretion of the court, hard labor not to exceed six months. (Knowledge of disease not required.)
Arizona	Misdemeanor	Anyone who knowingly exposes another person to an infectious or contagious disease in a public place or thoroughfare except as necessary in the removal of such person in a manner least dangerous to the public health is guilty of a "Class 2" misdemeanor. Punishable by a fine of not more than $750 or imprisonment not to exceed four months. (Knowledge required.)
California	Misdemeanor	Any person infected with any venereal disease or any person in-

Table 2 (continued)

State	Type of Crime	Provisions of Law
California (cont.)		fected with a venereal disease in an infectious state who knows of such condition and who marries or has sexual intercourse is guilty of a misdemeanor. Punishable by imprisonment in the county jail not exceeding six months and/or a fine not exceeding $1000. (Knowledge required.)
Colorado	Misdemeanor	Unlawful for any person with knowledge or reasonable grounds to suspect he has VD willfully to expose or infect another. The offense is a misdemeanor, and upon conviction punishment is by fine of not more than $300 or by imprisonment in the county jail for not more than 90 days or both. (Knowledge required.)
Delaware	Misdemeanor	Unlawful to expose another to infection. Fine up to $1000 and/or imprisonment up to one year. (No knowledge required.)

Table 2 (continued)

State	Type of Crime	Provisions of Law
Florida	Misdemeanor	Unlawful to engage in sexual intercourse when afflicted with any venereal disease. Offense is a misdemeanor in the second degree, punishable by imprisonment not exceeding 60 days and/or fine of $500. (Knowledge required.)
Idaho	Misdemeanor	Unlawful to expose another person to infection of venereal disease. Punishable by a fine of not more than $300 and/or by imprisonment in the county jail for not more than six months. (Knowledge required.)
Louisiana	Misdemeanor	Unlawful to infect another person in any manner or to perform any act that will expose another to infection. Penalty for the first offense, fine of not less than $10 or more than $200. For the second offense, fine of not less than $25 or more than $400. For each subsequent offense, fine of not less than $50 or more than $500 or imprisonment for not less than ten days

Table 2 (continued)

State	Type of Crime	Provisions of Law
Louisiana (cont.)		or more than six months or both. (Knowledge not required.)
Montana	Misdemeanor	A person infected with a venereal disease shall not knowingly expose another to infection. Punishable by imprisonment not to exceed six months in the county jail and/or fine not to exceed $500. (Knowledge required.)
Nevada	Misdemeanor	No person having a venereal disease in an infectious stage shall conduct himself in any manner likely to expose others to infection. Punishable by imprisonment in the county jail for not more than six months and/or fine of not more than $1000. A sentence of community service may be imposed in lieu of fine and/or imprisonment. (Knowledge required.)
New Jersey	Misdemeanor	No person having a venereal disease in the infectious stage shall en-

Table 2 (continued)

State	Type of Crime	Provisions of Law
New Jersey (cont.)		gage in the nursing or care of children or the sick; engage in the preparation, manufacture, or handling of milk, milk products, or other foodstuffs; work or be permitted to work in any dairy, creamery, milk depot, or any place where foods are exposed or handled; engage in any other occupation where infection can be transmitted; or conduct himself in such a manner as to expose others to infection. Penalty is a fine of not less than $10 or more than $100 for each offense. (Knowledge required.)
New York	Misdemeanor	Unlawful for any person knowing himself to be infected with an infectious disease to engage in sexual intercourse. Punishable by imprisonment of more than 15 days and less than one year and/or fine to be determined by the court. (Knowledge required.)
North Dakota	Infraction	Knowing exposure of venereal disease to an-

Table 2 (continued)

State	Type of Crime	Provisions of Law
North Dakota (cont.)		other is an infraction. Punishable by a maximum fine of $500. (If defendant has been convicted of another infraction within the previous year, he may be sentenced as if offense were a "Class B" misdemeanor, punishable by a maximum penalty of 30 days imprisonment and/or a fine of $500.) (Knowledge required.)
Oklahoma	Felony	It is a felony after becoming infected with venereal disease and before pronounced cured by a physician (in writing) to marry another person or to expose any other person by sexual intercourse. Punishment is confinement to the state penitentiary for not less than one year and not more than five years. (No knowledge required.)
Oregon	Misdemeanor	No person having any venereal disease in the infectious stage shall expose others to infection or engage in nursing or care of children or the

Table 2 (continued)

State	Type of Crime	Provisions of Law
Oregon (cont.)		sick or in any other occupation of such a nature that the disease can be transmitted to others. The offense is a "Class C" misdemeanor. Punishable by a fine of $500 or imprisonment for not more than 30 days. (Knowledge required.)
Rhode Island	Misdemeanor	Any person found guilty of knowingly exposing another to infection of venereal disease is subject to a fine of not more than $100 or imprisonment for not more than 30 days. (Knowledge required.)
South Carolina	Misdemeanor	Unlawful to expose another to infection of venereal disease. Following conviction, penalty is fine of not more than $20 or imprisonment for not more than 20 days. (Knowledge required.)
South Dakota	Misdemeanor	It is a "Class 2" misdemeanor for anyone infected with VD to expose another person to infection. Punishable by 30 days in prison in county jail and/or $100

Table 2 (continued)

State	Type of Crime	Provisions of Law
South Dakota (cont.)		or both. (No knowledge required.)
Tennessee	Misdemeanor	It is a violation to expose any person to infection. Punishable by a fine of not less than $25 and not more than $500. Each violation shall be a separate offense. (Knowledge not required.)
Texas	Misdemeanor	Knowing exposure of another to infection is a "Class B" misdemeanor punishable by a fine not to exceed $1000 and/or confinement in jail not to exceed 180 days or both. (The new law includes genital herpes in the definition of venereal disease but specifically excludes the transmitter of herpes from criminal sanctions.)
Utah	Misdemeanor	Knowing or willful introduction of any communicable or infectious disease into any county, municipality, or community is a "Class A" misdemeanor. Punishable by a term in prison not

Table 2 (continued)

State	Type of Crime	Provisions of Law
Utah (cont.)		exceeding one year and/or a fine of $1000. (Knowledge required.)
Vermont	Misdemeanor	Sexual intercourse while knowingly infected in a communicable stage is punishable by a fine up to $500 and/or imprisonment for up to two years. (Knowledge required.)
Washington	Gross misdemeanor	Unlawful to expose another to infection of venereal disease. Punishable by term in county jail for not more than one year and/or fine of not more than $1000. (Knowledge required.)
Wyoming	Misdemeanor	Law imposes civil liability on transmitter for infection of contagious disease and requires compensation to victim for all expenses including sickness, loss of time, and burial expenses. Fine of not more than $500 and/or imprisonment in county jail not exceeding six months. (Knowledge required.)

Note: A state-by-state guide listing complete health code statutes and penalties appears in Appendix III.

WHAT DO THESE LAWS MEAN TO ME?

In states that have criminal sanctions, a person who feels victimized by a sexual partner can file a complaint with the district attorney along with or instead of a civil action against that partner. The district attorney then decides whether there are sufficient grounds for arrest or indictment. In criminal cases, the burden of proof must be more substantial: the criteria of "beyond a reasonable doubt" must be met.

There are several reasons for filing such a complaint. The most obvious is revenge, plain and simple. Conviction of a crime provides a victim with redress for injury without instigating a time-consuming and costly civil case that may win the plaintiff damages that may be impossible to collect if, for instance, the defendant has no money. Such criminal action is therefore a vicarious form of relief for the victim because the defendant is prosecuted by the *state* and not by the victim.

For wealthy defendants who can easily pay big damages, criminal sanctions and the risk of criminal liability and jail sentences would no doubt be a far greater deterrent than even a large but unpublicized out-of-court settlement.

Second, for the victim who also wants civil redress for infection, the fact that there is criminal liability may help to facilitate civil claims. In Wyoming the law specifically imposes *civil liability* on those found *guilty* under the criminal STD statute. The law even requires compensation to the victim for all "expenses incurred by reason of such sickness."

Even without such specific provisions, in states that have a criminal statute, it is easier for a plaintiff in a civil action to meet his or her burden of proof. In these cases a plaintiff would not have to prove that the transmitter was negligent, only that a defendant violated the statute, because the majority of courts find that the violation of a statute enacted for the protection of the public is *negligence per se*. (See Chapter Two.)

The courts will reach that conclusion if three elements are present:

1. The plaintiff falls within the category of persons the statute was designed to protect.

2. The harm caused the plaintiff matched what the statute was designed to prevent.

3. The defendant breached the statute.

If these criteria are met, the defendant will be found to have been negligent. What remains for the courts to decide is whether there was contributory negligence or assumption of risk on the part of the plaintiff.

A final reason for filing a criminal complaint is public spirit. The purpose of the STD statutes is to protect public health and limit the spread of disease. Criminal accountability is undoubtedly a serious deterrent for people who might otherwise have little compunction about lying to their partners or infecting them.

CAN STATES REGULATE OTHER AREAS OF OUR SEXUAL CONDUCT?

Two other sets of laws affect the legal aspects of sexually transmitted diseases: those concerning fornication and sodomy.

If prostitution is the oldest profession, fornication (sex between unmarried persons) must be the oldest crime. The common-law crime of sexual intercourse between an unmarried man and an unmarried woman has been a preoccupation of the legal system in this country since the colonial era. In pre-Revolutionary Massachusetts, of 370 criminal cases brought before the courts, 210 were for fornication.

In 1965 fully 40 states still outlawed casual sex between unmarried partners. Offenders are rarely prosecuted unless they happen to be caught in the act in public places (beaches, parked automobiles, etc.), yet in 1987 fornication remains a crime in at least 15 states and the District of Columbia.

WHAT ARE THE RULES ABOUT FORNICATION?

Fornication in most statutes is defined as copulation—ordinary and uncomplicated sexual intercourse—between unmarried heterosexuals.

Although the rules seem out of step with social reality and current sexual mores, the majority of courts still uphold statutory punishments for fornication. The rationale is that a state may encroach on personal liberty upon showing a compelling state interest. That interest has been described as the need to prevent the birth of illegitimate children and curtail the spread of STDs as well as to prevent illicit intercourse.

But changes seem to be in the making. Many lawmakers are urging that these statutes be altered. The American Law Institute, for example, has called for the decriminalization of fornication. At least two states, New York and Pennsylvania, have struck down laws that regulate sexual activity between consenting adults.

In New York, where the fornication law was invalidated, the court remarked that the statute "mocks the dignity of both offenders and enforcers. . . . More importantly, the liberty which is the birthright of every individual suffers dearly when the state can so grossly intrude on personal autonomy."

Despite this, however, and despite constitutional challenges of privacy and denial of equal protection, so far fornication statutes continue to be upheld by American courts. There have been recent decisions in several states where courts rejected a defendant's contentions that consensual and heterosexual intercourse between two adults is within a protected area of privacy and cannot be regulated by state law. In these cases, the courts ruled that enforcement does not violate the right of privacy protected by the due process clause of the Fourteenth Amendment to the U.S. Constitution. Therefore, sex between unmarried partners is still held to be illegal.

This illegality has been used as a defense when one lover sues another for STD infection. But here we come to an interesting inconsistency: Although technically it is a valid defense, in this context it has been regularly overruled by courts, allowing one partner to sue another for tortious infection.

Fornication and Criminal Offenses

Penalties for the crime of fornication range from low-level misdemeanors to felonies. (A complete listing of state statutes and punishments appears in Appendix III.) Fornication is a crime in the following states:

District of	Illinois	North Carolina	Utah
Columbia	Massachusetts	North Dakota	Virginia
Florida	Mississippi	Rhode Island	West Virginia
Georgia	Minnesota	South Carolina	Wisconsin
Idaho			

WHAT ABOUT CONSENSUAL SODOMY?

Laws making sodomy or "unnatural sexual relations" a crime have been part of the English (and later American) common law since the sixteenth century. Before that such acts were a religious offense punishable in the ecclesiastical courts.

The earliest laws basically regarded only anal copulation as sodomy. Modern statutes, however, vary considerably in the kinds of sexual practices they prohibit. Often sodomy laws outlaw all oral-genital relations, bestiality, and other acts. Generally, the sodomy statutes encompass any human sexual activity that is "not natural." Apparently, the definition of "natural" in the legal context is heterosexual intercourse involving the penetration of the female vagina by the male penis.

Twenty-three states have abolished the laws against sodomy by legislative action. Three additional states, New York, Pennsylvania, and Massachusetts, have changed the law as a result of court decisions. Decisions are currently pending in courts in Arizona, Arkansas, Louisiana, Michigan, Minnesota, Nevada, and Texas.

The recent landmark decision in *Bowers* v. *Hardwick,* however, may throw a wrench into a consensus on the unconstitutionality of laws against sodomy. In *Hardwick* the U.S. Supreme Court validated Georgia's sodomy law as constitutional. The facts are relatively simple compared to the dramatic impact the Court's decision may have on future privacy challenges: On August 3, 1982, a policeman arrived at Michael Hardwick's home in Atlanta, Georgia, to serve a citation for failing to pay a municipal ticket. Hardwick's roommate pointed out his bedroom to the officer, who, opening the door, saw Hardwick engaged in fellatio with a male partner and promptly arrested him for violating Georgia's sodomy law.

The code states that "a person [who] performs or submits to any sexual act involving the sex organs of one person and the mouth or anus of another . . . shall be punished by imprisonment for not less than one year nor more than twenty years."

The Fulton, Georgia, district attorney declined to prosecute the case, but Hardwick filed suit in federal court, seeking an injunction and declaratory judgment that the law violated his civil rights. Hardwick's case was dismissed by a lower court, ruling that the sodomy law was *not* unconstitutional. The Eleventh Circuit Court of Appeals disagreed, and on Georgia's appeal, the High Court agreed to hear the case.

The Supreme Court decision confirmed that the state's "compelling state interest" gave it the right to regulate consensual sodomy and generated a storm of criticism. Some people fear it will have a profound negative effect on future regulation of private sexual conduct between adults. Others claim the decision is based on a fear of AIDS and an interest in controlling homosexual behavior. The opinion did not reveal how the Court would rule had it been a heterosexual couple involved in the proscribed act.

However, other legal experts seem to feel that the impact of this decision may not be as severe as some contend, for two reasons. First, individual states can rely on their own constitutions to remove laws regulating sexual behavior between consenting adults; second, courts have increasingly taken the position that regardless of existing laws—and this concerns the ability of one person to sue another when both are committing illegal acts—an injured partner has the right to recover damages if knowingly infected by an incurable disease during sexual activity.

Nevertheless, the infamous "crime against nature" is at present still good law in nearly half the states and the District of Columbia. Sodomy involving consenting adults in private is not illegal in most European countries. Sodomy has been legal in France since 1810. The United States and the Soviet Union remain the two major Western nations that still make the practice a crime.

In states where sodomy is a felony, the offense carries substantial criminal penalties. The laws are enforced even today, and stiff penalties including long jail terms are not found to be excessive or to constitute cruel and inhuman punishment within the perimeters of the Eighth Amendment.

CRIMINAL SANCTIONS FOR SODOMY

In many states sodomy is considered a crime. In a number of them it remains a felony. In Mississippi, for example, the offense is punishable by ten years in prison. In other states the penalty is a monetary fine. (Refer to the Appendix for a complete listing of state statutes and penalties.)

Sodomy is a criminal offense in the following states:

Alabama	Louisiana	Rhode Island
Arizona	Maryland	South Carolina
Arkansas	Michigan	Tennessee
District of Columbia	Minnesota	Texas
Florida	Mississippi	Utah
Georgia	Montana	Virginia
Idaho	Nevada	Wisconsin
Kansas	North Carolina	
Kentucky	Oklahoma	

The stiff criminal penalties still imposed for sodomy seem out of step with the sexual revolution. This imbalance has been made even more profound by the recent Supreme Court decision in *Bowers* v. *Hardwick,* which reflects a conservative turning point in legal thought. The right to privacy and the right of individuals to control their intimate associations is a still-evolving constitutional issue. Some analysts believe the Hardwick decision is due directly to an overreaction to the AIDS crisis.

AIDS and the Criminal Law

Criminal action by officials is today most likely in AIDS-related cases. Prosecutors have started filing criminal charges against suspects with AIDS for a variety of offenses. Here is a sampling of charges filed so far.

• An AIDS sufferer who sold his blood was charged with

attempted murder in Los Angeles. Edward Markowski admitted that he sold his blood between two and 23 times since learning that he had AIDS. This was the first murder indictment for selling contaminated blood in the nation.

- The Army may court-martial a Fort Huachuca, Arizona, soldier suspected of having sexual intercourse while knowing he was infected with the AIDS virus. This seems to have been the first time someone was charged with a crime for exposing a partner to the AIDS virus during sex. Private Adrian Morris, Jr., was charged with having had sexual relations with a female soldier and with a male soldier without revealing that a blood test showed him to be infected with HIV.

- An AIDS victim in Flint, Michigan, was charged with assault to commit murder after he allegedly spit on two policemen when he was arrested for a traffic violation. A judge later threw out all charges.

- A man in San Francisco believed to be infected with the AIDS virus pleaded guilty to misdemeanor assault charges and was sentenced to a 90-day jail term for biting a police officer. Prosecutors dropped plans to charge the man with felony assault after investigators discovered that the policeman who had been assaulted was homosexual and had a former lover with AIDS.

- In Minneapolis a prison inmate who has AIDS was indicted by a federal grand jury for assault with a deadly weapon (his mouth and teeth) when he bit two prison guards at a federal medical center. In June 1987 inmate James V. Moore was found guilty and faces a sentence of ten years in prison. The jury found Moore guilty despite the fact that neither prison guard tested positive for the AIDS virus and despite the fact that the prosecutor himself stated that it was not known if the AIDS virus could be transmitted through the saliva (*New York Times,* June 25, 1987). Moore was not charged and convicted under a public health communicable-disease law.

- In Texas prostitutes who are infected with AIDS face third-degree felony charges if they continue to engage in illicit sex.
- Health officials in several states have warned persons with AIDS that they risk criminal prosecution and imprisonment if they engage in sexual intercourse. These officials threaten to prosecute individuals through the use of the state's communicable-disease statutes, which make it a crime knowingly to transmit the disease. The Public Health Department in San Antonio has sent letters to AIDS victims warning them of potential criminal liability if they spread the disease.

Such incidents have raised the specter of routine referral of AIDS-related cases to the criminal courts under state communicable-disease statutes. In at least one state, Oklahoma, it is a felony to infect another person with a venereal disease. The crime is punishable by imprisonment of up to five years.

Officials involved in these cases treat the illness of AIDS as if it were an offensive weapon. Prosecutors and law enforcement officers contend that because of the risk of spreading the fatal disease, felony charges are appropriate.

Doctors and law enforcement personnel, however, disagree over the real health risks inherent in these cases. Many AIDS experts contend that the overzealous response seen in some of these criminal charges is a reaction to public hysteria about the disease and has little to do with an actual public health threat. This, in fact, was the claim of James Moore's defense attorney in Moore's recent conviction in Minnesota.

Despite assurances by health officials and medical experts that the disease is not spread through casual contact, the perceived threat by the public will no doubt result in the increased enforcement of state communicable-disease laws.

Politicians have also entered the arena, voicing their opinions about what should be done from a legal standpoint to curb the spread of the disease. Others share New York governor Mario Cuomo's views on AIDS, as reported in the New York *Post* (June 2, 1987):

If you know you have AIDS and deliberately pass it on to someone who is not aware, that should be regarded as a very serious offense. We're not talking about sins or morality—that you judge for yourself. I'm talking about sins against the community, a crime.

The governor's recommendations are now under consideration by state lawmakers.

In California, Congressman William Dannemayer has announced his belief that infection with AIDS should be a punishable criminal offense. In ABC's "National Town Meeting on AIDS," the congressman stated that in California public health laws have forbidden the transmission of STDs since 1957. "AIDS should be treated no differently," he said. The communicable-disease statute in California, like the law in New York, does not specifically list acquired immune deficiency syndrome as a venereal disease.

Nor, however, does it list genital herpes, and a recent court decision involving the transmission of genital herpes shows that this absence will not be considered a valid defense. The defendant in that case claimed that because genital herpes was not listed in the state's communicable-disease statute, it was not considered a "venereal disease." Therefore, the defendant claimed, it was not a crime to transmit the disease even through tortious conduct. The California court of appeals made its position very clear. It stated that even though genital herpes was not specifically named in the state's communicable-disease law, it is venereal in nature, and when the disease is spread by sexual contact, such transmission breaks the law. The court stated:

> Respondent's argument that genital herpes is not a venereal disease is unpersuasive. Although herpes is not listed among the "venereal disease" covered by the Health and Safety Code [in California] (specifically sec. 3001), that section was enacted in 1957, long before herpes achieved its present notoriety. We are not inclined to bar appellant's cause of action on the basis that genital herpes is not a venereal disease. It is a disease that can be propagated by sexual contact. Like AIDS it is now known to the public to be a contagious and dreadful disease.

At the core of this action is the misrepresentation of defendant that he did not have a contagious disease that could be passed to his partner. If a person knowingly has genital herpes, AIDS or some other contagious and serious disease, a limited representation that he or she does not have a venereal disease is no defense to this type of action.

The court's comment makes it clear that in the state of California diseases like genital herpes and AIDS are intended to be included in laws that penalize the transmission of STDs. Most states would most likely follow this same reasoning.

CRIMINAL OFFENSES

There are a variety of traditional criminal offenses that *theoretically* relate to the AIDS virus. The purpose of this discussion is not to encourage criminal complaints against persons with AIDS; it is intended to serve as an analysis of the criminal law and how it can relate to cases involving the disease.

Overzealous law enforcement officials and AIDS experts both agree on one thing: The best way to stop the spread of AIDS is education and prevention through behavior modification. Some analysts believe that changes in behavior can best be accomplished through the application of criminal law enforcement. Still others say that the criminalization of the transmission of AIDS could hinder the fight against the disease because those at risk may hesitate to come forward for counseling and treatment.

Whatever one's position, a general understanding of the criminal law and how it might relate to incidents involving persons with AIDS is vital. Knowledge is always the best defense.

The Various Offenses

In rare instances, *murder* might be charged against a person who infected another and this resulted in death. There are four distinct categories for murder (criminal homicide):

1. Intent to kill
2. Intent to cause serious bodily harm

3. Depraved-heart murder
4. Felony murder

Intent to kill means that a person consciously wants to kill another and does so or acts in such a way that death is inevitable. For instance, if a person is aware that he has AIDS, knows that infection with the disease will result in death, and deliberately and willfully infects another individual, he is theoretically guilty of intent-to-kill murder. The transmission of the disease could be accomplished by sexual intercourse, the sharing of contaminated intravenous drug needles, or transfusion of blood.

Intent to cause serious bodily harm is an unintentional killing that results from an act meant to cause severe physical injury. The element of malice must be present. In an AIDS situation this might mean that a person, knowing he had AIDS, forced another to accept a drug injection with a contaminated needle. The transmitter is aware that the injection can cause great bodily injury but is unaware that it could result in death.

Depraved-heart murder is an unintentional killing evolving from conduct that shows wanton indifference to human life and conscious disregard of the risk of death or serious physical harm. It indicates extremely negligent behavior and is considered criminal homicide. This could include situations where the AIDS carrier engaged in sexual intercourse or the exchange of bodily fluids without full disclosure of his medical condition. It could also encompass cases where a person shares an IV needle when he knows that such activity is likely to result in infection. Intent to kill is not required.

Felony murder is an unintentional death caused during the commission of a dangerous felony, such as burglary, rape, or arson. This would be the case, for instance, when a burglar shoots a police officer who happens on the scene of the burglary. The concept might be applied to the AIDS situation if an AIDS-infected person committed rape. If the victim of the crime later died from infection with the disease by the rapist, the defendant could be charged with felony murder.

There are several other categories under which an AIDS carrier might be indicted. If a carrier is *unaware* of the risk of virus-spreading contact and it results in the death of another human being, this can be grounds for a charge of *manslaughter*. Manslaughter in most states is defined as the unlawful killing of another without malice, express or implied. The act can be either voluntary, in a sudden heat of passion, or involuntary. The killing is done without deliberation, without forethought or planning. Manslaughter is a lesser offense than the intent, recklessness, or gross negligence required in the other murder charges. Thus a prosecution for manslaughter could be instituted against an AIDS carrier who was unaware that his conduct could lead to the spread of the virus.

Manslaughter charges would be most likely in instances where drug users failed to appreciate the risk inherent in sharing contaminated needles. It could also be invoked against a sexual partner who was unaware of the risk of spreading the virus through sexual intercourse. The offense is less than the willful, wanton, and reckless conduct required for criminal homicide but more than mere indifference to the rights and safety of others.

A charge of *criminal assault* could also be maintained against a sexual partner who transmits the disease. This charge would be based on the theory that where one sexual partner consents to engage in intimate activity, that consent is not full and informed if the other partner has failed to disclose that he is infected with the AIDS virus. The absence of full disclosure vitiates a partner's consent, and the resulting contact and infection could warrant charges of criminal assault. A sexual partner who has found himself in this kind of situation can file a complaint against the transmitter, and the district attorney will investigate. After investigation, the district attorney's office will seek charges against the suspect if appropriate.

SPECIAL CONSIDERATIONS

Causation

Whatever the charges, the prosecution must always prove that transmission of the disease is attributable to the defendant. The most difficult problem encountered in such cases would be proof of causation (see Chapter Five). The prosecution would be required to prove *beyond a reasonable doubt* that the defendant was the source of the AIDS infection.

This would require showing that the victim did not become infected with the disease in some other manner and that the victim did not engage in other high-risk activities that could have resulted in infection.

In cases involving intent-to-kill murder, this would require demonstrating the defendant's *mens rea* (guilty state of mind)— the deliberate and intentional killing of another human being. Proof of this kind of intent would be very difficult. In most situations it would be extremely difficult to prove both causation and culpability of the transmitter. Successful prosecution for this type of homicide in the great majority of situations would be unlikely.

Attempt

In cases where the victim has not died as a result of infection, a charge of attempted murder may be appropriate. These cases would involve persons who know they have AIDS and realize that sexual intercourse threatens risk of infection. Unlike the situation in homicide, death of the victim, cause of death, or even transmission of the virus would not be required. "Attempt" to transmit the infection is all that is required.

Violent Crime

The fear of contracting AIDS is so pervasive that, sadly, it can reach murderous proportions. There have been reports of people exploding in acts of violence after being informed that a sexual partner had the infection.

In one especially tragic case the reaction ended in murder. The failure of Kenneth Grice to tell a sexual partner that he had AIDS resulted in Grice's death. Lorenzo Owens, a 20-year-old Long Island, New York, youth, slit the throat of his homosexual lover minutes after they had anal intercourse and his partner confessed that he had AIDS.

The defendant based his defense on a "heat of passion" theory.

Owens told police that he was so outraged over his sex partner's disclosure that he immediately wanted to kill him. The case drew the intense attention of gay rights groups who feared that if Lorenzo Owens were acquitted, it would foster irrational and violent responses in similar cases. Nassau County Judge Richard Delin found little reason to be lenient with the killer—especially in view of the fact that Owens had sexual intercourse with his girlfriend soon after the murder—and sentenced Owens to 7 to 21 years in jail.

5

Causation: "How Can They Prove It Was My Fault?"

Multiple Sexual Partners

Causation is anything that produces a certain effect—the actual act that leads to an effect. As applied to the legal aspects of STDs, it means that when someone sues an ex-lover for infection, the plaintiff must show causation, that is, must provide sufficient evidence that the defendant was in fact the source of infection. Where other partners are involved, such proof becomes difficult.

What is required in such cases is to show *proximate causation*. In legal terms, that means showing not only who physically transmits the disease but also the person ultimately responsible for that transmission—what is termed "extended liability."

Proximate causation—that which produces injury or damage by an act or failure to act—is an important issue when more than two parties are involved. Just how far does a lover's responsibility extend? For example, if John transmits herpes to Mary, who subsequently transmits it to Bill, John's act would be the actual cause of Bill's herpes. Whether John's act was also the *proximate* cause of Bill's harm becomes a question of law for the court to decide.

The answer to that question hinges on a number of things. The first of these is Mary's knowledge that she had the disease *before* she slept with Bill. Four points will be considered: (1) Did John disclose to Mary that he had an STD before they had sex? (2) If he did not, did he tell her afterward? (3) Should Mary have known for other reasons, such as obvious physical signs? (4) Or did Mary find out in some other way that she had been infected?

If Mary knew or should have known that she had been infected by John before she slept with Bill, John is not liable for Bill's infection. If Mary did not know that John infected her, John is liable to Mary for the negligent transmission of disease. But is John also liable to Bill when Mary later spreads the disease to him? The answer to that question involves, in addition to the points just discussed, the legal doctrine of *foreseeability*. This is a crucial point, and the whole concept of extended liability turns on the questions of foreseeability.

WHAT IS FORESEEABILITY?

What kind of foresight should John have exhibited? Venereal disease is highly contagious. A person who has sex during an infectious period runs a substantial and foreseeable risk of infecting his or her sexual partner. And unless theirs was a strictly monogamous relationship, John can reasonably assume that Mary will have other sexual partners.

Is John therefore legally responsible when Mary later infects Bill? Did John have any legal *duty* with respect to Bill? In determining that duty, foreseeability plays a dominant role.

Negligence (see Chapter Two) is conduct that falls below the standard established by law for the protection of others against unreasonable risk. This involves a *foreseeable risk,* a threatened danger of injury, and unreasonable conduct in proportion to that danger. If a defendant could not reasonably be expected to foresee any injury or if a defendant's conduct was reasonable in light of the circumstances, there would be no negligence and no liability.

But if a defendant fails to act reasonably against harm he should have foreseen, how far will his legal liability extend? If Mary contracts genital herpes from John and then sleeps with all the players on her school's football team, is John liable to all of Mary's partners who subsequently contract the disease? Can John be hauled into court by each member of the team?

The ability of courts to limit liability based on foreseeability is illustrated in cases involving "open" automobiles. In these cases, a defendant negligently leaves the car keys in the ignition. The car is stolen, and the thief later injures the plaintiff in a serious auto accident. A majority of courts would find that although the defendant was negligent in leaving the keys and should have foreseen a theft, the defendant *could not* have foreseen that a thief would negligently harm the plaintiff.

If, however, a defendant leaves his car facing downhill and fails to set the brakes, he *can* foresee (1) that the car will roll downhill and (2) that it is likely to smash into someone or something and cause harm. In such a case the defendant should have foreseen the accident and will be held liable for any harm resulting from it. To illustrate these principles as they apply to STDs, if John did not inform Mary of his infection, he was negligent toward her. If, however, it can be shown that he had reason to believe Mary would *not* sleep with others, he would not be liable for Mary's infecting these other partners. By contrast, if it can be shown that John knew Mary to be promiscuous, he should have foreseen that she would infect other partners, and therefore John may be found negligent toward these others.

Limits to Extended Legal Liability

INTERVENING CAUSES

The courts use specific criteria in determining liability. Under the common law, if there was no special relationship between the parties, there was no duty on the defendant's part to control the conduct of third parties so as to prevent harm caused to a plaintiff. For instance, a defendant would have no duty to the plaintiff for injury caused by a thief, despite his own negligence, because the thief's negligence was an *intervening* unforeseeable act that cut off the defendant's legal liability. Courts generally find that a defendant could properly assume that third parties would not act negligently.

An analogous situation arises with John and Mary. John might foresee that Mary will have sexual contact with someone else. However, if Mary was made aware of her condition before sleeping with new partners, John should *not* be held to foresee Mary's *subsequent negligence* in transmitting the disease to another lover or even to the school football team. If courts follow this reasoning in John's jurisdiction, John would be liable *only* to Mary in negligence. Mary's subsequent negligence (sleeping with the football team after she knew or should have known of her medical condition) breaks the chain of causation and would be an intervening cause. The football team, obviously, can individually pursue legal action against Mary.

Even if an individual fails to disclose his condition and infects a sexual partner, an infinite number of intervening causes can still occur before the disease is ultimately transferred to a third party. Present-day courts tend to treat causes independent of a defendant's conduct (a third party's subsequent negligence) as relieving a defendant's liability if they are *unforeseeable* results of a defendant's negligent behavior.

NATURAL CONSEQUENCES

One test courts apply in assessing extended liability is to ask whether the resulting harm was a natural, probable, and foreseeable consequence of a defendant's conduct. Even if a result (infection with disease) is a direct result of the transmitter's conduct (failure to disclose his infection), liability exists only for the *natural* and *probable* consequences that can be reasonably foreseen.

In our case the court will have to judge whether the "natural" consequences of John's failure to tell Mary about his genital herpes would result in the infection of third parties (Mary's additional sex partners). It will be up to the court to judge whether John had foreseen that the virus, once transmitted to Mary, would be passed on to others. If it finds infection of the football team a natural and probable consequence that John should have foreseen, John may be found liable in negligence to such third parties.

Compare our hypothetical case to the rules regarding intoxicating minors. Most courts allow a third party to sue for injuries sustained through the negligence of a drunk minor against the person who sold or provided the young person with the alcoholic beverages.

The facts at hand are similar. John (the transmitter) knows that Mary is unaware of his infectious condition. Similarly, the bartender or party host knows that the minor is unaware of his intoxication. The bartender knows that a drunk minor is incapable of driving home safely—is likely to have an accident. John knows that Mary is likely to transmit the disease unknowingly to a third party.

In *Mary* v. *John* the court will determine whether John should have foreseen that Mary would *unknowingly* transmit the virus to another sexual partner. If Mary is ignorant of the danger, she is not accountable. Think of it this way: If John threw a live grenade to Mary, who, unaware of the danger, diverted it by tossing it to Bill, and as a result Bill is injured, all legal liability must remain with John, who originally tossed Mary the explosive.

When Does a Lover's Legal Liability End?

Once manifestations of the disease develop in the partner (Mary), and she knows or should know that she has the disease, legal liability for the original transmitter (John) ends.

In other words, if Mary, after sleeping with John, develops symptoms of genital herpes, visits a physician, applies prescription medicine, and then sleeps with Bill or the football team without disclosure while knowing she is infectious, Mary's conduct would be considered extraordinary. Her behavior falls below that of the reasonable person, and John's liability is cut off by Mary's superseding negligence because he could not foresee such negligence. Once Mary discovers that something is wrong with her physically, she must make every effort to obtain diagnosis and treatment and make full disclosure to new partners or abstain from sexual encounters.

If Mary fails to disclose her condition to a new sexual partner, legal liability shifts to her. John cannot be sued by Mary's lovers who later develop the disease. This is called a *superseding cause*.

SUPERSEDING ACTS

William Prosser in *The Law of Torts* describes superseding causes as "extraordinary forms of negligent conduct, . . . against which the defendant [is] under no obligation to take precautions."

As in the cases involving the negligence of a person who leaves the car keys in the ignition of his automobile and should have foreseen the theft, the subsequent negligence of the car thief is so extraordinary (and unforeseeable) that it cuts off the automobile owner's legal liability. The negligent operation of the motor vehicle by the robber is a superseding cause that shifts negligence from the car owner to the car thief.

Although John is still accountable for his own negligence toward Mary, he is not legally responsible for her later negligent conduct.

Proving the Source of Transmission

THE BURDEN OF PROOF

On the issue of causation, as on other issues central to a cause of action in negligence, the plaintiff has the burden of proof. The injured plaintiff in STD litigation must introduce evidence that would lead a jury to the reasonable conclusion that it is *more likely than not* that the conduct of the defendant was the cause of the plaintiff's harm. In our hypothetical case, Mary must prove by a preponderance of the evidence that John infected her with genital herpes.

A mere possibility of causation is not enough. Mary must provide a reasonable basis for the conclusion that John's conduct was in fact a cause of her infection with the disease. Mary is not required to prove her case beyond a reasonable doubt. It is enough for Mary to introduce evidence from which reasonable persons might conclude that it is more probable than not that the infection was caused by the defendant (John).

Mary can introduce circumstantial evidence, expert testimony, or common knowledge to prove her case against John. She can invoke the help of experts where their testimony involves information not within the common knowledge of a typical jury. On medical matters within common knowledge, no expert testimony is required to permit a conclusion as to causation.

A plaintiff who has been infected with gonorrhea or syphilis can generally prove the source of transmission through medical testimony verifying the dates of a defendant's infection and the dates of sexual contact with the plaintiff. Because syphilis and gonorrhea are generally curable, an investigation can pinpoint a precise span of time during which transmission of the disease took place—except, presumably, where the defendant fails to seek a cure. Depending on the facts of each case, proving causation in cases involving these two diseases can be established through expert testimony and medical records.

In cases involving genital herpes, however, establishing causation can be more difficult. The disease is incurable and recurrent, and there have been documented cases of asymptomatic transmission (infection with no discernible symptoms) by persons who have had the herpes virus but never had any symptoms or an outbreak of the disease. Such an asymptomatic carrier can and does infect partners, and this has been used as a defense where the carrier has infected a partner. This defense may work if it is genuine. If, however, the plaintiff can show, through relevant medical records or other convincing proof, that the carrier ever had the disease or symptoms of it, no matter how long ago, or had any reason to suspect that he or she had the disease, this defense won't work.

Nor can a defendant argue that a plaintiff already had the disease if physical symptoms show otherwise. A defendant who tries to argue that a plaintiff had earlier been infected by another partner will find himself defeated on the issue of causation if doctors testify that the plaintiff is experiencing a primary episode.

Because of the current epidemic of genital herpes in the sexually active population, defendants often counterattack that a plaintiff has been promiscuous and that even though the parties may have engaged in sexual intercourse, the defendant was not the actual source of the plaintiff's disease.

New medical technology facilitates the discovery of the source of genital herpes transmission with a degree of certainty unknown before, and in the future defendants will have a difficult time denying liability. So for the defendant who claims that "she can never prove it was *me*," if a new DNA fingerprint test proves positive, the defendant will have to take the blame and may find himself legally accountable in a court of law.

RESTRICTIVE ENDONUCLEASE ANALYSIS: THE DNA FINGERPRINT TEST

Noted herpes virologist Dr. Bernard Roizman of the University of Chicago states that at least half a million distinct herpes virus strains exist, each with a unique molecular structure. With a new tracing mechanism, called DNA restrictive endonuclease technology, scientists can positively identify a particular strain of genital herpes (HSV) from all others and can trace its spread within a population. Because of this medical progress, transmission of genital herpes is now provable. Thus it is now possible for experts to "fingerprint" the virus that has been transmitted through its DNA fragment patterns.

It is not necessary for a person to be experiencing an attack in order to be diagnosed with the disease. If tests initially prove positive, viral isolation can be used to determine the source of transmission. At worst, if circumstantial evidence and a DNA fingerprint test prove inconclusive, an isolated virus specimen may have to be taken from an active lesion. This way, causation can be shown conclusively.

A plaintiff in STD litigation can compel a defendant to submit to blood tests and a physical exam before trial. The results of such testing and the defendant's medical records from his own physician will generally indicate when a defendant had the disease. This information combined with witness interrogatories (written answers to questions under oath) and statements by the defendant given in a deposition (oral answers under oath) will indicate if the defendant was infected with the disease and whether he could have transmitted it to the plaintiff.

Third-Party Litigation

What seems to be the first third-party herpes suit, following the lines of our hypothetical case involving John, Mary, and Bill, was filed in Kentucky in March 1984. The complaint alleged that the plaintiff, a University of Louisville law professor, was infected with herpes after having sexual intercourse with his wife, who had previously had a love affair with the defendant, a local lawyer.

The plaintiff, Professor Leonard R. Jaffee, is seeking $250,000 from the defendant, Steven Wade Dills. According to the *National Law Journal* (May 7, 1984), the case has "caused a stir at the University of Louisville Law School and at the county courthouse, where clerks have done a brisk business making photocopies." In the lawsuit Professor Jaffee charged that the defendant had sex with his wife in the spring and summer of 1983 without telling her that he had the disease. The plaintiff alleged that because of Dills's "fraudulent, willful and wanton misrepresentation," his wife was infected with the disease, and after they were reunited, he contracted it too.

In his answer, defendant Steven Dills admitted the affair with Mrs. Jaffee but denied misrepresenting his medical condition or transmitting the disease. There does, in fact, seem to be some question as to whether the defendant failed to disclose his contagious condition to the plaintiff's wife. There seems to be evidence indicating that Mrs. Jaffee was aware of Dills's condition. If so, the plaintiff would have little hope of collecting a judgment in negligence because Dills's extended liability would be cut off by the subsequent negligence (nondisclosure to her husband) of the plaintiff's wife.

To avoid these problems of extended liability, lawyers for Professor Jaffee have not filed an action in negligence but seek relief for the ancient tort of "criminal conversation" (in which a third person is held responsible for sexual relations with a spouse's husband or wife) and are seeking damages for "alienation of affection and consequential damages for the contraction of herpes." In other words, the plaintiff claims that his damages (contraction of genital herpes) were a result of the defendant's "wrongful interference" with his wife.

To support a judgment for the tort of criminal conversation, a plaintiff must prove that he and his wife were validly married and that sexual relations took place between the defendant and the plaintiff's spouse. Such tort action is based on the common-law doctrine that a husband has an exclusive property right in his wife, and when another man engages in sexual intercourse with her and violates that right, criminal conversation occurs.

In Kentucky adultery (in which legal action would take place between the spouses) is no longer a crime, but criminal conversation is still good law. It enables a person to sue a spouse's lover for extramarital sexual relations. Few states still support the tort, and Kentucky has not heard a case charging criminal conversation since 1968, when an Appalachian woman was awarded $10,000 after a jury found she had been wronged by her husband's mistress.

In the past courts have permitted recovery for criminal conversation even when the adulterous spouse consented to the adultery or even initiated it. The basic argument is founded on the idea that one spouse cannot consent to behavior that would harm the interest of the other. Legal scholar William Prosser, in *The Law of Torts,* makes this statement:

> The idea that one spouse can recover for an act the other spouse willingly consented to is perhaps better suited to an era that regarded one spouse as the property of another, and at least one court has suggested that in such a case only nominal damages might be allowed and some judges have opposed the action altogether.

Legal experts comment that such third-party action is a "logical outgrowth" of a nationwide epidemic. Robert Rabin, a Stanford University law professor who has followed the proliferation of STD litigation, called the suit "the first of its kind," but "a logical next step beyond herpes cases we have now."

Definition of Infectious Periods

The time during which STDs are contagious varies by disease. For the length of time that an individual has a contagious medical condition he also carries the legal responsibility of safe and reasonable conduct. The sufferer must abstain from sexual contact when necessary or take appropriate precautions. And—a crucial point for legal protection—he or she must always make full and complete disclosure of relevant medical history to any intimate partner.

No expert testimony is required for a jury to make conclusions as to matters within common knowledge. Obviously, any juror could decide, based on matters within common knowledge, that visible signs of venereal disease indicate a contagious period and that a defendant should know better than to engage in sexual conduct that could transmit the disease.

In such cases the plaintiff may be found to be partly at fault (see the discussion of contributory negligence in Chapter Six). However, a jury is likely to show little compassion for the defendant who has knowledge of the disease yet engages in reckless behavior anyway.

Expert testimony may be required, however, where medical matters outside the common understanding of the jury are relevant. With STDs that are less well known or where diagnosis and symptoms are more complicated, experts inform the court about the medical facts and infectious periods.

Cases involving syphilis and gonorrhea are straightforward. Symptoms are readily recognizable, the diseases are familiar, and court cases relating to them are generally clear-cut. Once causation is established, a jury will assess damages according to the facts of each individual case.

Other infections, such as chlamydia, condyloma acuminata (genital warts), and genital herpes, are less familiar in their medical characteristics. The AIDS virus is now receiving widespread media attention. New technology and scientific research can help the court's ability to understand some of the distinguishing characteristics of each of these diseases, and in such cases experts are often called in for guidance.

Let's take a systematic look at six of the STDs dealt with in this book and some of the special considerations involved in each type of infection for the purposes of STD litigation. Early symptoms for each disease were described in Chapter One. Bear in mind that the key issues in these cases are not only intent—did the defendant *know* he had the disease?—but also the definition of the infectious period—was the defendant contagious when he had sex with the plaintiff?

GONORRHEA

What is generally not known about gonorrhea is that transmission can occur without sexual contact by exposure to vaginal discharge and saliva. The period of infection starts at the very first symptoms and ends only when the disease is completely cured, as vouched for by a doctor. A partner who is infectious must, in order to avoid all potential legal liability, abstain from any sexual contact whatever. Even the use of a condom cannot guarantee complete safety, because the contraceptive device does not adequately protect all areas of the body from contact with the infected secretions.

This is a debilitating illness, causing chronic pelvic inflammatory disease and closing of the fallopian tubes; the disease is thus a major cause of sterility in women. Women who ultimately become sterile as a result of the willful or negligent transmission of gonorrhea can seek substantial dollar damages.

Gonorrhea is caused by the gonococcus bacterium. This organism can live in the mouth and be passed by casual kissing. When symptoms occur, the sufferer must not engage in oral sex or simple kissing. Even with full disclosure, the risk of transmitting the disease is so great that abstinence is mandated morally and legally.

It is estimated that there are 1.6 million new cases of gonorrhea in the United States each year. In a sexually active population, the disease spreads rapidly, and new antibiotic-resistant strains are now being encountered in the United States. While there are said to be effective ultra-broad-spectrum antibiotics available in Japan, they are not yet authorized by the federal Food and Drug Administration for use in America.

The good news is that with early detection and treatment the common types of gonorrhea are completely curable. Once gonorrhea is effectively treated, its transmission to others is prevented. Complications arising from the disease are not uncommon, however, and could win the victim a considerable sum in damages, as in the case of Margaret Housen (see Chapter Three). Although Ms. Housen later lost the award because of a technicality (an expired statute of limitations), the legal doctrine is certain: Lovers who fail to disclose that they have gonorrhea are accountable in a court of law.

If at present you have an untreated case of gonorrhea, you must abstain from all sexual contact, even casual kissing. After the condition is cleared up with prescribed antibiotics, revisit the doctor and get a clean bill of health with an exam and a lab test. Following notice by your physician that you can safely engage in sexual intercourse, inform a new partner that you once had the disease and give the dates. Take whatever precautions are necessary, and consider using a condom. Be on the lookout for similar signs in the future that you may have been reinfected with the disease.

SYPHILIS

Historically, syphilis has been one of mankind's great curses, and there has been a pervasive fear of it over the ages. Many notable people have suffered and died from its effects. One was the father of Winston Churchill, who contracted it in the course of a practical joke while in college. The prank, sadly, involved an infected prostitute.

Syphilis leads to the general physical and mental deterioration of the victim since it affects all systems of the body, especially the nervous system. The disease is carried by tiny organisms called spirochetes, which are transmitted during sexual activity. It is infectious from the time the organisms invade the body until treatment with antibiotics is complete and blood tests are negative. The blood test must be repeated by your doctor every three months for two years. Otherwise you may have the disease in a silent phase, which is damaging to you and very dangerous to your partner.

Before syphilis was curable, transmission of the disease meant serious, lifelong illness and often early death. Damage awards early in this century to victims against former lovers who infected them reflected the serious, irreversible consequences of exposure to the disease. Lacy Crowell's $10,000 award from her syphilitic husband was a huge sum of money in 1910. Courts were willing to take drastic punitive measures against defendants who willfully infected their spouses, and in 1917 Harry Lankford was found guilty of criminal battery and ordered jailed by the court when he deliberately infected his wife with the painful and then incurable disease.

If detected at an early stage today, syphilis can be successfully treated with antibiotics. But the disease remains insidious because the symptoms can disappear after the initial infection. The primary lesion can heal and even with treatment the disease can remain active and undetected in the body for years. Unless the person has a blood test specifically for the disease, it may continue to develop unnoticed and untreated through the second and into the third phases. It is increasingly difficult to treat in the second stage. In the third stage, the infection can be arrested with antibiotic therapy. However, the profound damage to many of the organ systems in the body cannot be reversed.

The best way to deal with syphilis both medically and legally is to have routine blood tests for it, especially if you are sexually active, because it is easily eliminated with early detection and proper antibiotic treatment.

If you have *ever been exposed* to the disease or you think you might be experiencing symptoms, it is your *legal responsibility* to ask your doctor to administer the appropriate tests during frequent medical checkups. As with gonorrhea, to avoid any risk of legal liability, simply abstain from all sexual contact, oral or genital, during the contagious phase and until the condition has entirely subsided. Check with your doctor before engaging in sexual intercourse following treatment for the disease. Tell a new partner of your experiences. Be aware of the legal consequences if you should intentionally or recklessly infect another person with the disease.

CHLAMYDIA

An estimated 4 million Americans, mostly young heterosexuals, will contract chlamydia this year, making it the most widespread STD in the nation. Because health regulations in many states do not yet require reporting cases of chlamydia, the Centers for Disease Control's estimate is considered too conservative, and some researchers fear that the actual number may be as high as 10 million. "We are in the midst of a chlamydia epidemic," says Dr. Thomas Quinn of the National Institute of Allergy and Infectious Diseases.

Chlamydia can best be described as a silent epidemic. Many sufferers are unaware that they have the condition, and most have never been tested for it. That is why the legal considerations involving chlamydia are distinguishable from, say, genital herpes or gonorrhea, where symptoms are clearly visible and apparent. Many people who are infected with chlamydia are genuinely unaware of it, and when charged with fraud or failure to disclose the condition, they can argue that they had no idea they were contaminated but honestly believed they were suffering from the flu or exhaustion or even a persistent urinary tract infection.

Chlamydia is a bacteria-like disease that attacks the reproductive system in women, often exhibits few symptoms, and can lead to painful pelvic inflammation, miscarriages, and sterility. It also increases the risk of ectopic pregnancies—when the fertilized egg settles outside the womb—and newborns can be infected by mothers with the undiagnosed disease. A test has only recently been developed. Women are often not tested until the disease has progressed and patients are confronted with such symptoms as painful urination, vaginal discharge, abdominal pain. This is a pity because despite its high resistance, the diagnosed disease can be treated with antibiotics and definitely eliminated.

This disease can take its emotional and physical toll on patients, which can have an important impact on compensatory damages in a judgment for a successful plaintiff.

Often people with chlamydia are genuinely ignorant that they are carriers. Even so, plaintiffs have successfully sued partners who have infected them. To avoid any legal liability, watch for symptoms that put you on notice that you should visit your doctor for testing and treatment until you have a clean bill of health.

Chlamydia is often overlooked or confused by physicians with many other conditions, such as trichomoniasis, yeast infection, and bacterial vaginitis. The disease is highly contagious, and detection is a major problem. In some cases the organism can apparently live in the genital tract of women for many years. Men usually have no symptoms of the disease but can be silent carriers and transmitters. Patients must constantly be alert to new outbreaks and consult their doctor.

The woman in Dallas won a verdict of $375,000 based on divorce and personal injury claims when she was able to prove that her husband infected her with chlamydia after he had been infected by his lover in an extramarital affair. The husband, who showed no signs of the disease, was a silent carrier and transmitter. As a result of the infection, the plaintiff was rendered infertile.

Once detected, chlamydia is difficult to treat with antibiotics, and frequent relapses occur. In most cases two weeks of treatment are necessary, followed by testing to confirm the cure. Reinfection by untreated partners is very common, and male partners often resist examination and treatment.

Since the disease can be spread without sexual contact, it is almost impossible to wipe it out in a family without treating every member. It is thought to be transmitted through household activities via such ordinary means as contact with common towels and washcloths. Thus all family members must be treated.

There do not at present seem to be any lawsuits between members of a household for infection through nonsexual contact, but the legal basis on which to sue is available. Persons who intentionally or recklessly spread the disease, even by innocent contact, are accountable unless they take adequate safeguards and make full disclosure. Just as in cases involving tuberculosis or any other infectious disease that is spread nonsexually, a defendant can still be held liable whenever he acts below the standard of the reasonable person and contaminates others.

Some experts believe that the only way to stop the spread of chlamydia is by voluntary screening of high-risk groups, especially sexually active women with multiple partners. Doctors urge that more research is required but complain that chlamydia research has been sidetracked because of the growing emphasis on AIDS. Health care costs related to chlamydia and associated medical problems for the disease may total more than $1.3 billion a year, according to the Centers for Disease Control.

To avoid legal problems, ask your doctor about chlamydia and ways to reduce the possibility of contracting it. Sexually active individuals should take the initiative to prevent infection by selecting low-risk sexual partners and using barrier methods such as the condom and spermicide. Women who plan pregnancies should always be tested and treated before they become pregnant. Be aware of the symptoms and get regular medical advice.

If you are now being treated for the disease, you have a *legal duty* to inform all the members of your household and take extra measures to avoid the spread of the virus in your living and working environment. Inform all sexual partners of the problem, even after medical treatment.

GENITAL WARTS

Genital warts (condyloma acuminata) is another highly infectious, easily transmitted disease that has of late reached epidemic proportions: There are 1 million new cases each year in the

United States and the true extent and total number of cases is unknown. The large recent growth in reported numbers of patients with genital warts has created a problem for both patients and their physicians. Although folklore has it that most untreated warts disappear by themselves and that almost any treatment will achieve the same results, patients generally suffer with warts for many years with no permanent relief. They are of great medical importance because they can be spread through nonsexual contact.

The disease is found in the genitals of women—virgins as well as those sexually active—and affects the external genitalia, the labia, clitoris, introitus (opening to the vagina), and hymenal ring.

In both men and women, genital warts frequently occur inside the anus and thus, because they go unnoticed, are a common cause of treatment failure. These wart lesions may be found in every part of the body. They may be small, flat, barely perceptible irregularities of the skin, or they may be large growths that cover the genital area. They can lead to total incapacitation of the patient, causing intense pain, itching, bleeding, and burning, and can precipitate urinary and bowel obstructions that may require hospitalization.

Since warts are difficult to find and often cannot be detected with the unaided eye, the gynecologist must use special instruments like a colposcope with special magnification. Even with these instruments, however, it takes a well-trained and experienced physician to detect the presence of the very early, tiny lesions.

The warts are caused by the human papilloma virus. There is evidence that this virus can be transmitted by a person to different sites in the body, most frequently affecting the genitals. The virus has at least 45 variations that occur in different areas of the body. These include, in addition to the genital and anal types, plantar warts (on the bottom of the foot), elbow warts, finger warts, and scalp warts.

When the virus reaches the genital region of a woman, it is often one of the undiagnosed causes of frequent urinary tract "infections." Warts that occur in the mouth, nose, or throat have been very difficult to treat before the development of the CO_2 laser.

Researchers have come to believe that certain male and female genital cancers are closely associated with various types of the human papilloma virus. The virus is very resistant to treatment, reinfection can take place, and auto-infection is not infrequent.

Pregnant mothers can transfer the warts to the vocal cords of their infants during a vaginal delivery, and cesarean sections are necessary if the condition is present. Thus accurate diagnosis and treatment are of critical importance during pregnancy.

Genital warts, one of the most troublesome and ubiquitous of the viral venereal diseases, are a dangerous epidemic, and there is a distinct need to raise the consciousness of physicians and the general public to their danger. At the present time there is very little general or professional awareness of the problem.

The pain and inconvenience of the condition plus the new evidence linking genital warts to a precancerous condition make understanding of the disease and its prevention an important part of medical and legal care. With all the inherent problems involved with the disease, a direct effort not to spread it is imperative. Full disclosure in any sexual encounter is required. Safe practices to avoid infection include use of condom or spermicidal jelly, self-examination, and frequent gynecological evaluation.

AIDS

The signs of a health crisis of shocking proportions were apparent even before actor Rock Hudson died of AIDS in 1985. By any measure, control of the AIDS epidemic is an awesome task. In June 1986 the U.S. Public Health Service predicted that the number of AIDS patients would jump tenfold in five years, to almost 270,000 full-blown cases.

That report drew front-page headlines across the nation. The projections were startling, but even more disquieting was the fact that the figures were based on the number of Americans believed to have the antibody to the AIDS virus. This showed that they had been exposed—an estimated 1.0 to 1.5 million people—but had apparently not yet developed the disease itself. There is now evidence that the figures used by the Public Health Service were understated. New studies by the Centers for Disease Control indicate that AIDS cases were being underreported on death certificates by as much as 17 percent, apparently to spare victims' families embarrassment. The disease works by weakening the immune system and crippling the body's natural defenses to infection and cancer. The body then becomes the victim of an array of infections and rare disorders.

AIDS can be spread in three major ways: by sexual contact, by blood contact as occurs in intravenous drug use, and from mother to newborn child during pregnancy. A small percentage of cases are blamed on transfusions with HIV-contaminated blood products.

Here is the best way to avoid being infected by the virus:

- If you use injectable drugs, never share needles or equipment.
- If you are sexually active and have not been in a mutually monagamous relationship for the past ten years, to be safe, since medical opinion is not set on the subject, consider practicing low-risk sexual behavior.

According to guidelines issued by the Los Angeles City AIDS Task Force, sexual behavior can be categorized as follows:

High risk

- Intercourse without a condom
- Oral sex with climax in the mouth
- Contact with urine and feces
- Semen or blood in the mouth or on skin that has cuts or sores
- Oral or manual contact with the rectum
- Sharing of sexual devices

Medium risk

- Deep kissing
- Intercourse with a condom (which may tear or leak)

- Oral sex that ends before climax
- Contact with urine and feces on uncut skin

Low or no known risk

- Hugging
- Holding and cuddling
- Body-on-body contact
- Social kissing
- Masturbation and massage

Tests for the virus have been licensed by the FDA but contain a small margin of error: They reveal previous exposure to the virus by detecting antibodies but not the virus itself. Presence of antibodies is not proof that the patient will develop AIDS or ARC. However, individuals who test positive are considered to be infected and capable of spreading the virus to their sexual partners, even if the disease never develops to its hideous potential within them.

Researchers are not sure how many people who test positive will develop full-blown cases of AIDS, but estimates now predict at least 60 percent. Illness may occur five or more years after initial infection.

It is thought at this time that more than 80 percent of patients diagnosed as having AIDS will die within two years as their weakened immune systems are overwhelmed by diseases healthy bodies can easily resist. "Not since syphilis among the Spanish, plague among the French, tuberculosis among the Eskimos, and smallpox among the American Indians has there been the threat of such a scourge," the *Journal of the American Medical Association* warned in 1987.

With everything that is at stake with AIDS, it is almost inconceivable that a person would knowingly expose another to the deadly virus. Yet that is exactly what has prompted cases like Marc Christian's lawsuit against the estate of Rock Hudson.

Lawsuits brought against AIDS victims range from deadly assault to attempted murder. The irreversible consequences of the disease and its death sentence make infection morally and legally repugnant. Failure to disclose the condition is extreme and outrageous behavior far below the standard of decency imposed on a reasonable person to protect the health and well-being of others.

The individual can best protect himself medically and legally through safe-sex practices. Full disclosure of any relevant medical history—including intravenous drug use, multiple sexual partners, blood transfusions, and undiagnosed symptoms—must be conveyed to any lover. Talking honestly can save lives.

"Despite the best efforts of the scientific community, biomedical research cannot eliminate the problem of AIDS in the short term," Harvey V. Fineberg, dean of the Harvard School of Public Health, wrote in the *New York Times* in June 1986. "The fact is that we require no new technological breakthroughs to limit the spread of the AIDS virus." This view has been repeatedly confirmed by experts ever since.

The *Journal of the American Medical Association* is in agreement. "Individuals," it notes, "have the power to protect themselves more than science currently can." Emphasis in the future must be placed on education and prevention, not just medical research and intervention. Knowledge of legal liability and financial accountability to lovers and ex-lovers for harm caused through negligent or willful conduct is an important part of that prevention.

GENITAL HERPES

In its cover story on herpes in August 1982, *Time* magazine called the disease "today's scarlet letter." An estimated 40 million Americans now have genital herpes (herpes progenitalis), and the Centers for Disease Control report 500,000 new cases each year.

"The truth about life in the United States in the 1980s," says Dr. Kevin Murphy, a leading herpes researcher, "is that if you are going to have sex, you are going to have to take the risk of getting herpes." Herpes is hardly the worst venereal disease; untreated syphilis and gonorrhea can do far more physical damage. But unlike the other common forms of venereal disease, herpes is at present incurable. A popular joke describes the situation succinctly: "What's the difference between true love and herpes? Herpes lasts forever."

Emperor Tiberius banned kissing in Rome some 2000 years ago to stop a scourge of lip sores; herpes has been with us for a long time. But today's modern sexual aggressiveness has turned the disease into a new medical and legal epidemic. Although the infection cuts through all levels of society, 95 percent of herpes patients are Caucasian and 53 percent are college-educated. The affliction can have a profound impact on interpersonal relationships and can contribute to further medical complications.

The herpes simplex virus (HSV) is of two types: Type I causes fever blisters; type II gives rise to herpes progenitalis. Both types now occur in the mouth and genitals.

Once contracted, the virus travels through the nerves and settles in the spinal nerve root. Current knowledge indicates that it periodically reactivates under stress. However, it also seems to recur for causes that are still unknown. The infection can have numerous results:

- Blisters and pustules
- Sores
- Ulcerations
- Muscle aching and headache
- Localized breakdown of the skin
- Intense itching
- Severe pain
- Anxiety
- Fever
- Depression

While adults are more likely to spread HSV through intimate contact with another person, children with fever blisters have been known to spread the virus to their genitals accidentally with their fingers.

If you suffer from cold sores or fever blisters and engage in oral sex, there is a good chance that your partner can develop herpes in the genital area. Thus you must never engage in any sex when cold sores or any type of herpes lesions are present.

The fetus is at risk of infection if the mother has HSV. A cesarean delivery is often required to prevent exposure of the newborn to the genital infection. In addition, HSV is thought to increase the risk of cancer of the cervix.

Herpes can be spread through asymptomatic transmission (when the transmitter has no symptoms, may never have had either symptoms or an outbreak of the disease, and may be genuinely unaware of having it). Herpes can also be acquired asymptomatically, in which case the victim has the virus but may not have symptoms or an outbreak for months, years, or ever. This can complicate proof of the source of the infection (causation) in the event of a legal confrontation.

HSV is, however, detectable by a blood test. To make certain you are protected legally and medically, make periodic testing for the disease a routine during your physical checkups. Avoid oral-genital sex when either partner is contagious. Use a condom and virucidal contraceptive foam in between herpes outbreaks and at all other times. Whether you are currently contagious or not, it is *absolutely mandatory* to talk about it with any sexual partner. Your legal duty of care demands it.

Answer your lover's questions with candor and insight to prevent the spread of the disease, and help others with herpes adjust to the condition with the latest medical and legal information.

We have been bombarded with stories about the frightening results of the sexual revolution: the epidemic of genital herpes; increased occurrences of chlamydia, hepatitis, and genital warts; and, especially, the AIDS constellation of infection, pneumonia, cancer, and death. Even syphilis, one of the oldest venereal diseases, reached record high levels in the United States in 1987, increasing 30 percent over 1986.

Despite some of the media attention focused on the problem, we've had relatively little new information on what we can do to protect ourselves. That is why a general understanding of the legal ramifications of sexual intimacy is critical. The law is one protection that a lover can turn to in building a safe sexual relationship with his or her partner. Legal trouble for lovers who lie is delivered by a legal system that provides compensation for those who have been injured by the false promises of a sexual partner.

For some, recognition of the legal aspects of sexual intimacy has come too late—they are forced to seek relief against former lovers in the courtroom. For the rest, the news comes just in time—the gentle threat of legal action can spare a partner illness and anger when honesty is encouraged before all sexual encounters. Learning the legal fundamentals can protect everyone from the negligence or the greed of others.

An individual's decision not to share a contagious medical condition is no longer a personal matter. It becomes the basis of legal action for damages if a partner should become infected. In other words, sexual responsibility is mandated by law.

Over 14 million new cases of STDs are expected this year, and many of the victims will be young, career-minded professionals who date multiple partners. As the chances of catching or giving a disease mushroom, sex becomes a risky business for everyone.

What is at stake between sexual partners? The answer is not only medical risk but also the new threat of legal action. Be prepared and arm yourself with the information every lover needs to have.

6

Winning Damages

Some of the men and women who have gone to court and filed charges against former partners for transmitting an STD have made headlines. Some of the less sensational cases have changed the law. Their stories are moving and powerful. For many, it was not the award of money damages that motivated them to seek relief but the satisfaction of legal victory against a dishonest or immoral partner. The legal proceedings describe a conflict between the public good and private morality that may well become the dominant social issue of the 1990s.

But even for those who seek a moral victory against an ex-lover, a successful court verdict means dollar damages. Although injuries sustained by plaintiffs for the wrongful transmission of disease will differ considerably among individuals, one thing is certain: Infection is a physical injury for which the plaintiff is entitled to compensation.

Recovery in Negligence

COMPENSATORY DAMAGES

A plaintiff may seek recovery for three reasons:

- Loss of earnings and diminution of future earning capacity

- Medical and other expenses
- Mental pain and anguish (emotional distress)

In some cases, awards are also made for special damages. All are considered compensatory damages. Such damages are awarded to return the victim as much as possible to his or her condition prior to injury. Like any person found liable in negligence, the transmitter of disease is held accountable for *all foreseeable consequences* of his negligent conduct. The defendant can thus be held liable for all the past, present, and future results—both physical and emotional—of the nondisclosure of his contagious condition. *American Jurisprudence Second,* a legal encyclopedia, describes a typical negligence damage award:

> A plaintiff is generally *not limited* to the pecuniary losses which have occurred, but may also recover damages for future losses which will—in the opinion of the trier of fact—result from defendant's wrong. Further, compensatory damages are not necessarily restricted to the actual loss in time or money. They also include such as may be awarded for bodily pain and suffering, permanent disfigurement, disabilities or loss of health, injury to character and reputation, and, in most states, wounded feelings and anguish.

In STD cases, a successful plaintiff with a strong showing of proof can obtain compensation for all medical bills associated with the illness. These can include expenses already incurred and those that are reasonably certain in the future.

Where complications have arisen as a result of the disease— for example, sterility for women or serious complications associated with gonorrhea, syphilis, or condyloma acuminata—the plaintiff can, in addition, recover special damages. Such special damages are defined in *Black's Law Dictionary* as "those which are the actual, but not the necessary, result of the injury complained of, and which in fact follow it as a natural and proximate consequence in the particular case, that is by reason of special circumstances or conditions." This means that if a plaintiff suffers unusual complications that are the direct but not necessarily the typical result of the infection because of a particular reaction or sensitivity that may not normally occur in others, this plaintiff is entitled to an award of special damages. For example, Margaret Housen suffered unusual complications from gonorrhea due to an unusual physical susceptibility. Whereas a person normally would recover from gonorrhea after treatment with antibiotics, Margaret required, in addition, surgery and other costly medical procedures. Her complications were the "actual" result of the injury, but not the typical or "necessary" responses. Margaret was entitled to special damages as a result of the unusual complications she suffered.

The infected partner can also seek recovery for lost pay at work due to illness or visits to doctors and hospitals. Further, if a plaintiff has lost a job because of the disease (not uncommon in cases involving genital herpes), the plaintiff can seek compensation for reduced earnings in the future that are a direct result of the negligent infection.

For many plaintiffs the emotional injury can be more devastating than the physical one. Many courts now award compensation for emotional pain and suffering when it is established as a result of the physical injury. States like California permit recovery for anxiety about the future course of an injury. Such awards have been granted over worry about whether a dog bite can result in rabies or excessive X-rays will result in cancer. In one lawsuit against a dentist, a California court allowed damages to the victim of X-ray burns for the future threat of cancer. Defense attorneys objected that damages for anxiety over future harm were uncertain and conjectural. The judge stated that the necessity of continual monitoring against cancer was a burden on the plaintiff that the defendant had no right to inflict.

Situations involving STD cases are analogous. Condyloma acuminata has been documented to be a precursor in some cases of cervical cancer. Genital herpes can pose a potentially fatal threat to unborn or newborn infants of mothers with herpes. Vaginal delivery during active infection can result in catastrophic harm of infection to a newborn. Medical studies report that infant mortality rates are 50 percent, and surviving infants face increased chances of permanent sight or brain impairment. Doctors often advise delivery by cesarean section. Such anxiety over a future course of illness related to a defendant's negligence may be recoverable in courts that follow California's rule.

Even men with genital herpes reportedly suffer constant worry over future outbreaks, possible complications, embarrassment, and sexual dysfunction. But both men and women who have been wrongfully infected tell about the mental trauma associated with the disease.

Time magazine told of a Washington lawyer, aged 28, who spent a month in bed with her first bout of genital herpes, then stayed drunk for half a year. She divided her time between ritualistic repetitions of the phrase "This hasn't happened to me" and harsh daydreams of revenge against the man who gave her the disease. She stopped wearing makeup, ironing her clothes, and shaving her legs. "I felt as though someone had pulled the plug," she said, "and let all my sexuality and self-confidence swirl down the drain."

This woman's reaction is not uncommon. Although some people with the disease report little discomfort after the primary episode, others find themselves deeply scarred by the disease, physically and emotionally. Genital herpes is recurrent and cannot be cured. Given all these factors, the potential for substantial damage recovery is likely. A defendant is liable for the plaintiff's particular and unique response to the disease, both medically and emotionally.

Awards in cases involving syphilis and gonorrhea are likely to be more moderate except where a plaintiff suffers unusual complications from the disease. For instance, Margaret Housen's large original jury award reflected her unusual medical problems. The jury in the Texas case of the woman who was unable to have children as a result of negligent infection with chlamydia took that injury into account in its compensatory award of $375,000.

IF YOUR LOVER IS POOR: HOMEOWNER'S INSURANCE

Can a defendant turn to his or her insurance carrier for payment of STD-related claims? The answer in some cases is yes. Most homeowner's insurance policies and generally most standard renter's policies cover the insured for any "bodily injury" for which the insured may be legally liable. In a situation where a defendant has little money or no assets on which to collect a judgment, the plaintiff may look to a defendant's homeowner's insurance policy for payment of a tort-related claim.

A homeowner's insurance policy protects the policyholder against bodily harm, sickness, or disease the insured negligently causes others. A common claim under such a policy is for the familiar "slip and fall" accidents by guests in the insured's home. Food poisoning claims have also been brought against homeowner insurance.

Homeowner's policies will cover bodily injury due to an insured's *negligence* but exclude coverage for *intentional* harms. In order to recover, a plaintiff's claim must be based on negligence and not on any of the intentional torts like battery or fraud.

Plaintiffs have successfully settled with insurance carriers regarding cases involving the transmission of genital herpes in several major cities. One case reported in *Time* magazine involved a New York electrical worker who was sued by his former girlfriend.

> Like many lovers, Martin kept his infection a secret, which he later came to regret after ending his relationship with Debbie (not her real name), a secretary in her early 30's. He met Debbie in June 1985, and their affair was idyllic until early August, when she broke out in painful blisters around her vagina. After that, says Debbie, "the relationship deteriorated, and by Labor Day he dumped me and left me alone with a case of herpes."

Angered by being "treated very badly," Debbie hired a Manhattan lawyer. The attorney established that Martin, who had little money, was covered by a homeowner's insurance policy, making it possible to collect a judgment. At his deposition Martin admitted that he had not told Debbie about his infection. In March 1987 Debbie and Martin agreed to a settlement of $119,052 to be paid by the insurance company.

A Minneapolis woman who caught genital herpes from a sexual partner reached a $25,000 settlement with the man's homeowner's insurance company. Stewart Perry, the woman's lawyer, said his client "had no idea [the man] had herpes. The defendant knew he had herpes and he was negligent in giving it to her. But we couldn't claim he did it on purpose." A spokesperson for the insurance company, Prudential Property and Casualty Company, of Holmdel, New Jersey, said she knew of no other similar settlements by her company.

There have been other cases of insurance settlements for STDs, although carriers are hesitant to talk about them. As a result of the increase in STD-related claims, carriers have begun changing homeowner's policies to exclude claims for sexually transmitted diseases. Although this could have a dampening effect on future cases, many previously filed cases are moving through the court system with insurance policies that provide for "bodily injury" based on the negligent transmission of disease.

Does the sex act have to take place in the person's home for the policy to cover the incident? No. The policy will still cover bodily injury that occurred as a result of the policyholder's negligence. In most policies the term *bodily injury* includes the term *disease*. The insurance policy follows the insured like a puppy: Wherever the policyholder goes, and no matter where the sex acts take place, if contraction of an STD results from the negligence of the insured, the insurance carrier must make good on the policy.

Recovery in Battery and Fraud

PUNITIVE DAMAGES

In intentional tort cases (see Chapter Three) the plaintiff may also ask for and get punitive damages. These are intended to punish the wrongdoer and serve as a warning to others. A conscious disregard for the rights and safety of a sexual partner or a conscious indifference to consequences are the earmarks of a claim of punitive damages. These can be awarded where a plaintiff can demonstrate that a defendant acted with malice or willful indifference. In this context malice does not have to mean that the defendant deliberately set out to transmit an STD to his sexual partner. Malice can be inferred where the defendant knew he had the disease and was or should have been reasonably certain he would infect a sexual partner. If a defendant knows that he has the disease and carelessly engages in sexual intercourse with the plaintiff anyway, without disclosing his illness, infection is likely to result. Therefore, the defendant's actions may be sufficiently outrageous to warrant a punitive award.

Such damages are given to a plaintiff over and above full compensation for the injuries (compensatory damages). The exemplary (punitive) damages are sometimes called "smart money." Mere negligence is not enough to earn such damages because it lacks the element of spite, fraud, malice, or motive on the part of the defendant.

When appropriate, the jury can consider evidence of a defendant's wealth in assessing the dollar amount of such damages. The rationale is to make the sum large enough both to deter the defendant and to punish him adequately for his conduct.

The punitive award must, however, bear some reasonable relationship to the actual damages. A very small compensatory award may not support a huge penalty. But where a defendant's conduct is so outrageous that the particular circumstances call for it, very large punitive awards have been sustained even though they were out of proportion to the damage suffered by the plaintiff.

EXTREME AND OUTRAGEOUS CONDUCT

The deliberate failure to disclose infection with the AIDS virus may be the most outrageous and malicious fact pattern in STD litigation. Knowingly to expose another human being to a fatal virus is so malicious that it supports a strong punitive award.

A good example for such action is the suit brought by Rock Hudson's last lover, Marc Christian, against the Hudson estate. Christian charges that the late actor deliberately withheld the facts of his illness for nine months after learning that he had AIDS and in fact denied being infected when his lover specifically asked him about it.

Although Christian has not thus far tested positive for HIV, he claims that according to his doctors he is at severe risk of developing the disease at any time during the next five years. His attorney, Marvin Mitchelson, has stated repeatedly that his client's life has been endangered and that he now lives in constant fear that he might get the fatal disease. If Christian wins his case, considerable punitive damages would be appropriate. He is, in fact, asking for a total of $20 million in general damages for negligence, bodily injury, mental distress, fraud, and deceit from Hudson's estate and another $4 million from Hudson associates for conspiring with the actor to keep his condition a secret.

Additional Damages

AWARDS IN DEFAMATION (LIBEL AND SLANDER)

Defamation has remained a common-law offense. It includes libel, which originally concerned printed or written words, and slander, which was generally oral. Defamation is an attack on the reputation and good name of the plaintiff. It involves the opinion that others have of the plaintiff in the community. The elements of defamation are communication concerning the plaintiff that is communicated to a third person, is defamatory in nature, and results in damage to the plaintiff.

The *Restatement (Second) of Torts* provides the definition of defamation. A communication is defamatory if it tends to harm the reputation of another so as to lower him in the estimation of the community or to deter third persons from associating or dealing with him. Communication would tend to prejudice the plaintiff in the eyes of a substantial and respectable minority.

The determination of what kinds of statements constitute defamation is difficult. But courts have found that statements that a kosher meat dealer sells bacon, that a teacher is guilty of misconduct with his students, or that the plaintiff is a murderer can be defamatory under the right circumstances, that is, if they harm or disgrace the plaintiff.

It is not defamatory, however, to say that a person is dead, that he is overcautious with money, that he has led an uneventful life, that he has no known or permanent address, that he has the possession of the goods of another and owes him money, or that he is not entitled to communion in a particular church. Such language, if it is false and malicious, may provide a basis for another tort action (intentional infliction of emotional distress), but it lacks the element of personal disgrace required for defamation.

Because of the impact of the written word, and, in our day, of television or radio, it was accordingly held that some kinds of defamatory words might be libelous and actionable without proof of actual harm because of the *potential* harm they can cause. If the words, however, were spoken (slander), damage to the plaintiff must be proved—that is, slander is not actionable without substantiated harm to the plaintiff. The courts, however, early on established significant exceptions to this common-law rule. One of these concerns the untrue imputation of a "loathsome disease."

The rationale was based on the premise that after a person had been falsely accused of having a venereal disease, this person would be excluded from society. This exception to the proven-damage rule was originally limited to venereal disease and a few cases involving leprosy and was not applicable to disorders like smallpox or tuberculosis.

A false communication made by the defendant that a plaintiff is infected with an STD falls into this category in most courts, and a plaintiff can seek damages even when he or she cannot prove any actual harm.

Medical advances have made venereal diseases like gonorrhea and syphilis curable, and therefore some jurisdictions no longer rigidly abide by this rule. Some courts will find that a statement that a plaintiff has had VD in the past would not be sufficient to warrant an award of damages without some proof of harm. The reasoning is that the imputation of a former infection would not stir up the same social stigma. Courts will split on this issue, and whether they will find that defamation has taken place will depend on the facts. Some courts will ask for proof of special damages, in which case a plaintiff will need to demonstrate some pecuniary loss. Termination of employment or loss of job opportunities is sufficient.

But in most courts, if defamation regarding an STD can be proved by the plaintiff, that in itself is considered to establish the existence of some damage or injury to a plaintiff. The jury, even without other evidence, can estimate that harm in terms of a dollar amount. After defamation is established, the jury can take into consideration injury to the plaintiff's reputation, wounded feelings, humiliation, and any resulting physical illness or pain. The amounts awarded are left to the discretion of the jury and can vary widely, from 6 cents to six figures.

A Maryland cardiologist has sued a Baltimore hospital and launched a $35 million suit claiming that it allowed word that he had AIDS to leak out among medical colleagues and ruin his career. The doctor claims that he contracted AIDS through a cut on his finger when a glass tube of blood withdrawn from a patient broke. The lawsuit alleges that officials at Johns Hopkins University allowed word of the doctor's illness to spread among his colleagues. The physician can seek action against the hospital for invasion of privacy but will have little success in pursuing any lawsuit in defamation because the information, by the doctor's own admission, is true.

Defenses

ASSUMPTION OF THE RISK

A defendant charged with negligence can raise the plaintiff's contributory fault as a defense. Many defendants will charge that the plaintiff assumed the risk of exposure by sleeping with the defendant. Defendants may claim any of the following failures on the part of the plaintiff:

- Failure to inspect the defendant before having sex
- Failure to inquire about venereal disease
- Failure to wear a condom or insist that a condom be worn
- Failure to use virucidal contraceptive foam

The defense can assert that a lover assumes all the risks attached to sex, including the risk of pregnancy or the transmission of venereal disease, simply by consenting to sexual intercourse. One man charged with infecting his ex-partner with gonorrhea defended himself by saying, "Sex is a dirty business. Every schoolboy knows that."

When properly raised, "assumption of the risk" is a complete defense in trials where negligence is the issue. In STD litigation, however, where one partner has knowledge or should have knowledge that he has a disease, that same defense is not convincing. To be a valid defense, the injured partner must have appreciated and clearly understood the full nature of the risk before engaging in the ultimately harmful sexual activity. A victim who is unaware of her lover's condition cannot fully appreciate the risk she is undertaking.

Three elements are required to prove assumption of the risk:

- Plaintiff knows the risk is present.
- Plaintiff understands the full nature of the risk.
- Plaintiff enters into the risk voluntarily.

Without full knowledge of the risk she is accepting, a plaintiff has not assumed a thing. A plaintiff is never held to have assumed the risk of conditions about which she has no knowledge. A defendant's nondisclosure or recklessness prevents any full understanding of the nature of the risk involved.

Under certain circumstances the court may find that the plaintiff was *partly* at fault (for instance, by not asking the defendant about obvious physical signs of disease). If so, the plaintiff's award for damages would be reduced proportionately because of her comparative negligence. However, there is only one set of circumstances in which a defendant can defend himself with total success on the basis of a plaintiff's assumption of the risk. That is when the plaintiff, *following full disclosure by a defendant,* agrees to engage in sexual intimacy. In other words, if a party *knows* that another has a contagious disease, *understands the risk* of engaging in sexual intercourse, and absolves the lover of responsibility for possible transmission, this party has voluntarily assumed the risk and can no longer hold the defendant legally accountable.

In our hypothetical case, this would work out as follows. If Mary meets John, engages in sexual intercourse after John has told her he has an STD, and contracts that STD, she has assumed the risk and has no cause of action.

If John lied to Mary and told her he was free from infection, Mary has a cause for an action in fraud.

But if Mary did not ask and John did not offer the information, the jury would have to weigh the facts to decide whether Mary was also negligent. If it is found that Mary should have asked John about his sexual history, and by her failure to do this she was 20 percent at fault, her award for damages would be reduced by 20 percent. Additional findings of contributory negligence on Mary's part would further reduce the dollar amount of her award, perhaps, under certain circumstances, to nothing.

Many lovers with a contagious condition do describe it to a sexual partner. Such disclosure becomes a valid defense only if these criteria are met:

- Was the condition of a partner *fully disclosed,* with all its implications of risk?
- Did the other person *fully understand* the implications of engaging in sexual activity as well as the risks involved? That is, was this person sober and mentally competent and thus able to grasp the risks involved?

If these criteria are met, a defense of assumption of the risk will be successful.

When making full disclosure to a partner, make sure that he or she is not intoxicated and is able to understand the nature of the problem. When a partner makes full disclosure to you, if you choose to accept the risk, bear in mind that you have released your partner from legal responsibility. Be informed. Make the right decision for you. And to be really safe, put it in writing.

CONTRIBUTORY NEGLIGENCE

Are Both Partners at Fault?

Contributory negligence involves the concept of whether the plaintiff is also to blame. Under common law, if a plaintiff is found to be even 1 percent at fault (contributorily negligent), she is completely denied recovery because her conduct fell below the reasonable standard of care necessary for her own protection. Engaging in sex when presence of infection is visible or failing to ask when it is reasonable to do so could constitute fault on the part of a plaintiff.

The harsh doctrine prohibiting recovery when a plaintiff is partly to blame has been revised in many jurisdictions. This sweeping change in negligence law is known as "comparative negligence." In states that follow the doctrine, the contributory fault of the person injured does not prohibit recovery. Damages are simply reduced in proportion to the amount of negligence attributable to the plaintiff.

"Comparative negligence" was adopted in California in 1975 and has been followed in many other states. The principle has been used in STD litigation as well. The jury will determine what percentage of the blame lies with each partner, and the plaintiff will be denied damages attributed to her own negligence.

STATUTE OF LIMITATIONS

Each state has established a code of rules that set forth the time frame within which tort actions must be filed against a defendant. Failure to file within that time period can result in dismissal of the case. The statute of limitations for a personal injury lawsuit varies from state to state.

In some jurisdictions the statute begins to run only after the plaintiff has discovered the injury. In those states, in our hypothetical case involving Mary and John, Mary would have only whatever time the statute specifies in which to file a tort action after she had been diagnosed by her doctor or had reason to believe she had been negligently infected by John.

In some other states, a plaintiff will have a certain period (again specified by the statute) from the date of injury in which to file a complaint. No matter how grievous an injury, a plaintiff is out of luck and unable to pursue any legal relief if the statute runs out before she files legal action.

This happened in the case of *Duke* v. *Housen* (Chapter Three), in which the $1.3 million jury award was overturned on the basis of the expiration of the Wyoming statute of limitations. This was a technicality, but it forever prohibited the plaintiff from recovering any of her judgment against the man who recklessly infected her with gonorrhea.

The statute of limitations is especially troublesome in the case of AIDS, where the latency period between the infection and the development of antibodies is unknown. The presence of HIV cannot be determined until the body produces the antibodies. In addition, there is a long period between the development of antibodies and AIDS-related diseases; in fact, such diseases may never develop. And a person suspecting he might be infected and submitting regularly to tests may have the virus and yet it may not be susceptible to diagnosis.

This situation naturally poses grave problems for people who suspect they may have been infected—Marc Christian, Rock Hudson's lover, is a prime example. These people may often have to sue for emotional distress rather than provable physical harm.

Check the statute of limitations for personal injury lawsuits in your state and make certain that if you need to pursue any of your legal rights, you are not prevented from doing so based on the lapse of time. Defendants will quickly seize on an opportunity to challenge a lawsuit on the basis of a statute's expiration, and if the dates fall outside the permissible time frame, the lawsuit will be dismissed and the defendant can walk away without retribution.

The Issue of Privacy

Sexual intercourse is an intimate event. How far can the government reach when regulating and enforcing matters involving private, intimate associations?

Courts have long recognized the right of privacy in matters relating to marriage, family, and sex and accordingly have frowned on unwarranted governmental intrusion into matters affecting an individual's right to privacy. This issue has often been used by defendants trying to fend off actions by lovers they may have infected.

The right to privacy, however, is not absolute, and that is why it is usually rejected by the courts as a defense. It is a right that is subject to the overriding interest the state has in protecting the health, welfare, and safety of the people.

The right to sexual privacy is not explicitly mentioned in the U.S. Constitution. But the due process clause of the Fourteenth Amendment, which forbids the deprivation of "life, liberty, or property without due process of law," has been interpreted by the Supreme Court as broad enough to provide substantive protection against state infringement of a broad range of individual interests, including unwarranted governmental interference in matters of sexual privacy.

Anyone sued for the transmission of disease will have to be asked and will have to answer many personal questions. What was said in the bedroom? Who said what? Who did what? Defendants claim that judicial inquiry into these matters violates their constitutional right to privacy. The question then is when such inquiry serves the state's obligation to protect the public and therefore takes precedence over the individual's right to privacy.

Recent decisions in California courts have specifically addressed the issue of the right to privacy in intimate settings. The decisions in these cases illustrate the direction most U.S. courts will take when confronted with such issues.

In one unusual case, the plaintiff, Stephen K., claimed that before he and his lover had sex, she told him that she was taking birth control pills. Stephen said he relied on her false representation but that later his lover became pregnant and gave birth to a baby girl. In response to an action for paternity by the woman, Stephen sued for compensatory damages, claiming unwanted financial obligation and emotional distress concerning the child. He also sought an additional punitive award based on his partner's misrepresentations.

The California court of appeals dismissed Stephen's lawsuit, refusing to involve itself in the private and intimate activities of a couple engaged in sexual intercourse. It stated that the parties were asking the court to supervise the "promises made between two consenting adults as to the circumstances of their private sexual conduct. To do so would encourage the unwarranted governmental intrusion into matters affecting the individual's right to privacy."

In addition, "as a matter of public policy the practice of birth control, if any, engaged in by two partners in a consensual sexual relationship, is best left to the individuals involved, free from any governmental interference."

In a second case, *Barbara A.* v. *John G.,* a woman was told by her sexual partner that he was sterile. As a result of his false representation, the woman suffered a life-threatening ectopic pregnancy. The woman had consented to continued intimate relations based on this false representation. The trial court, relying on the decision in the case involving Stephen K., ruled that the woman did not have a valid basis for a lawsuit.

On appeal, however, a higher court found that the cases were very different and ruled in favor of the plaintiff. The court said that in *Stephen K.,* the damages concerned "wrongful birth" and parental child support, but in the second case there was a direct physical injury.

The appellate court stated that the right of privacy was "not absolute." The harm to Barbara as a result of tortious conduct by the defendant was serious and very real. Therefore, the right to privacy does not "insulate from liability one sexual partner who by intentionally tortious conduct causes physical injury to the other."

Barbara A. and the cases involving the transmission of STDs have strong similarities. The alleged tort is deceit (false representation), and the injury (ectopic pregnancy) was a direct result of sexual activity based on that misrepresentation. When a plaintiff sues her ex-partner for the transmission of VD, the false representation has also resulted in injury (the transmission of VD).

The reasoning in the case involving Barbara A. was the basis of a landmark decision in California regarding the nurse who contracted genital herpes as a result of her sexual partner's false statements. (See the discussion of *Kathleen K.* v. *Robert B.* in Chapter Three.) The court found that the deceit of the defendant resulted in the infection of the plaintiff. The intentional tort plus the state's interest in controlling the spread of "contagious and dangerous diseases" established a proper basis on which the plaintiff could institute legal action.

These decisions show that courts will not allow the right of privacy to protect defendants who infect others with STDs. Such conduct endangers the health of the community and inflicts physical injury on healthy sexual partners. The right of privacy is secondary to the important social interest of protecting the public health.

Courts are reluctant to sanction state intrusion into the privacy of intimate relationships, but they are willing to look at intimate matters in order to preserve justice. When and with whom sexual activity can take place should not be regulated, but there should be and is legal encouragement of honesty between sexual partners.

Therefore, defendants who claim that their constitutional right to privacy protects them from liability will find little support in the courts and will find that they have to pay for the wrongful transmission of disease. The pain and suffering inflicted on a lover and that lover's subsequent sexual partners far outweigh the defendant's right to privacy.

Lovers who are not honest about an infectious disease face legal liability and severe penalties if they do not comply with the important duty of disclosure. Be honest with your partner before sex. The privacy rights of the person who spreads STDs are not a good defense.

Considerations Before Launching Legal Action

A plaintiff engaged in STD litigation must be prepared to open up the most intimate aspects of his personal sex life. Once a defendant has been charged with the transmission of disease, his medical history becomes relevant and is a proper subject for court inquiry. Martin, the New York electrical worker, was required to answer a lawyer's repeated questions regarding the intimate details of his sexual activities. Defendants will be questioned about medical and sexual histories by interrogatories (written answers to questions under oath) and depositions (testimony under oath outside the courtroom). Lawyers for the plaintiff can obtain a defendant's medical records and in some cases can compel a blood test to determine the presence of disease. Lawyers asked Martin, for example, "Did you ever suffer from blisters or sores on your penis or genitals?" and "Did you ever have difficulty achieving or keeping an erection during sexual intercourse?"

Minnesota lawyer Stewart Perry, who has handled some of these special cases, states that clients must be prepared to have part of their intimate life opened up to public exposure. Deposition questions will be very personal and explicit. In some cases, however, Perry has succeeded in limiting the questioning of his clients regarding their sex life to only three months before the date of infection.

Clearly, this is not a course of action for persons who shy away from highly personal revelations. Even those who do not will have to be strongly motivated.

7

STDs: Legal Rights and Responsibilities

People afflicted with sexually transmitted diseases—especially those suffering from herpes or AIDS—have increasingly found themselves discriminated against in most areas of their lives. They have found such discrimination in employment, housing, health care, insurance—in short, everywhere, including their social life.

Little can be done to legislate a more benign, open-minded attitude in social settings. However, activity has been increasing to control discrimination in other areas. The federal government and most states now have laws barring dismissal of employees on the basis of physical disability, and STD infections are increasingly being considered in that category. All 50 states and the District of Columbia have enacted some form of unfair trade practices legislation, which controls the insurance risk classification process; this legislation prohibits discrimination between similarly situated persons where rates, policies, or benefits payable are concerned. These laws concern only unfair discrimination. They still implicitly acknowledge that insurance companies have the right to determine what constitutes risk in line with the premises on which their business is built.

Discrimination resulting from STDs knows no barrier. It is directed at sufferers of all ages.

Employment Discrimination

The Herpes Resource Center, a California-based national service of the American Social Health Association, has reported numerous cases involving discrimination against workers who have genital herpes. The center described the conflict in its monthly newsletter, *The Helper* (Summer 1984):

> In January of this year, the owner of a small restaurant phoned the Herpes Resource Center for some information and guidance. The dilemma he faced involved an employee who had recently been accused by his fellow workers of having genital herpes. These employees were demanding the man's resignation for fear that if he stayed they too would catch the disease. The owner himself admitted that he was concerned, fearing that his customers could acquire the disease from the employee when he greeted them or brought them food.

The newsletter went on to recount a similar case of discrimination against a young real estate worker who was fired after her first attack of genital herpes. At first she'd been told that her job performance was inadequate, but when this was challenged, she was told the real reason for the firing was fear that she'd infect her fellow workers.

The center receives many such reports from across the country and says, "It is our contention that a single case of threatened job security or loss of employment is one instance too many."

The cases described by the Herpes Resource Center involving employment discrimination are not unusual. Individuals in many cities have been terminated from employment because they have a sexually transmitted disease. Persons with AIDS and genital herpes apparently suffer the worst kind of discrimination and harassment. What legal means does an individual have to protect his or her job?

On the federal level the Vocational Rehabilitation Act of 1973 prohibits federal contractors and recipients of federal funds from discriminating in employment on the basis of a handicap. The law was enacted to combat stereotypical prejudice and ease the handicapped worker into mainstream activities. It applies to discrimination in employment, housing, and education and also covers all employees of the federal government.

Who is a "handicapped individual" under federal law? According to the Health and Human Services (HHS) regulations, a "physical impairment" under the act is "any physiological disorder or condition, cosmetic disfigurement, or anatomical loss affecting one or more of the following body systems: neurological; musculoskeletal; special sense organs; respiratory, including speech organs; cardiovascular, reproductive, digestive, genitourinary; hemic and lymphatic; skin and endocrine."

The employer is also required to accommodate handicaps to a "reasonable" extent. Employers who violate the Vocational Rehabilitation Act face several possible penalties. Generally, a victim of employment discrimination can seek job reinstatement and back pay. Employers may also find their federal financial assistance suspended or terminated.

When adopting the definition of physical impairment, the HHS expressly refused to set forth a specific list of the diseases that constitute a physical impairment or handicap. Since the law was enacted, appellate courts have applied it to cases involving heart disease, blindness, epilepsy, multiple sclerosis, and diabetes. The question of whether contagious diseases are also covered on the federal level has never been directly tested until recently. Theoretically, a sexually transmitted disease could be interpreted as a "physiological disorder" that affects the hemic and lymphatic systems.

Does the federal law cover persons with contagious diseases? The issue has now been decided by the U.S. Supreme Court in a case involving a teacher who was fired because of her infection with tuberculosis. The Court held that contagious diseases are handicaps within the meaning of the federal law. The case is of national importance, and experts predict that the Court's decision will eventually be construed to apply to STDs like AIDS. If so, it will then be illegal to fire public employees on the basis of such disabilities. This may then also trigger relief for all persons who are discriminated against because they have an STD.

Although there is no uniform national law that governs disability discrimination in private and public jobs outside the jurisdiction of the Vocational Rehabilitation Act, nearly every state has laws forbidding such discrimination: Fully 42 states and the District of Columbia cover both the private and public sectors, five only the public sector. The three remaining states, Arizona, Delaware, and Wyoming, have no such laws.

AIDS-RELATED EMPLOYMENT DISCRIMINATION

What should an individual do when he suspects that he has been a victim of employment discrimination? In one of the first cases testing this issue, an employee of Broward County, Florida, was fired after county officials discovered he was a carrier of the AIDS virus. Todd Shuttleworth, 33, received a termination letter from his employer four months after his diagnosis. The letter stated:

> There is no factual dispute regarding the reason for your termination. Upon confirming that you were diagnosed as having Acquired Immune Deficiency Syndrome (AIDS), the county took the position that in order to protect its employees and members of the public with whom you could come into contact in the performance of your job functions, your future employment would pose a potential risk to others.

Shuttleworth filed an appeal with the Florida Commission on Human Relations on the grounds of unlawful employment discrimination. Florida became the first state agency to hold that AIDS is a protected "handicap" within the context of employment. The commission ruled that an unlawful employment practice had occurred when Broward County discharged Todd Shuttleworth from his job to protect coworkers from exposure to AIDS. In view of the lack of credible evidence supporting the employer's fear that AIDS is transmitted by casual contact in the work environment, this fear was found to be insufficient to fire the employee.

Todd Shuttleworth won a $190,000 settlement and was rein-

stated in his job. The settlement compensated Shuttleworth for
back pay, medical bills, and legal fees. "It's a tremendous victory
in our leading case," said Nan D. Hunter, a lawyer for the American Civil Liberties Union.

The case suggested that the county's actions violated state and
federal laws that prohibit discrimination. Unless an employer can
demonstrate a reasonable danger by the continued employment
of an AIDS victim, the presence of employees with AIDS will
not likely be held to constitute an unacceptable health risk to
coworkers or clients to justify their exclusion or termination.

In an article on Todd Shuttleworth's victory, the *New York
Times* quoted Urvashi Vaid, a lawyer and spokesperson for the
National Gay and Lesbian Task Force. The settlement, Vaid said,
"sends a strong message to employers across the country that
people with AIDS cannot be discriminated against, that they
must be treated as if they had any other handicap."

Of all STD-connected discrimination, the most prevalent is
against AIDS sufferers. The statistics report the increasing legal
problems presented against the person with AIDS in all areas of
civil rights including housing, school, and employment. That is
why several states have enacted laws specifically prohibiting discrimination against people with AIDS, and others are likely to
follow.

Because medical authorities do not believe AIDS can be transmitted through casual contact, the presence of employees who
have AIDS is not considered an unacceptable health risk to workers or customers. Employers who exclude AIDS patients from
the workplace solely because of the disease may violate the Rehabilitation Act of 1973, because the Department of Labor Office
of Contract Compliance considers AIDS patients disabled under
this statute. Nevertheless, the Justice Department, in June 1986,
said that federal law did *not* prohibit refusing to hire people with
AIDS if employers were reasonably fearful of the health and
safety of other workers. The issue has been addressed by the Supreme Court with regard to one contagious disease, tuberculosis.
Application of the law as to AIDS and other STDs may be the
next step.

Can workers with AIDS be expected to perform in the work-place? Medical experts say yes. The Centers for Disease Control in Atlanta issued a report stating that "employees with AIDS should work to the extent of their physical capacity." Accordingly, it is illegal for most federally funded employers or employers with government contracts to fail to "reasonably accommodate" AIDS patients who are able to work.

Other civil rights laws protect workers with AIDS against discrimination. Various state laws, such as the New York Executive Law (Sec. 296), prohibit discrimination on the basis of disability. Los Angeles has explicitly prohibited discrimination against AIDS patients or any group perceived to have AIDS in housing, education, and employment.

THE DUTY OF THE EMPLOYER

AIDS in the workplace presents serious legal and moral issues to the employer who must confront the conflict. Employers must manage their business while accommodating the rights of AIDS victims with the rights of employees and customers who fear exposure to the disease. The situation illustrates the enormous conflict between an individual's civil rights and the public health needs of the nation and applies to STDs in general.

What are the rights and obligations of employers with respect to AIDS?

- May an employer ask applicants whether they have AIDS?
- If so, may the employer ask only particular applicants, or must the employer ask all applicants?
- May an employer test workers for AIDS?
- May an employee be fired because he or she has AIDS?
- If employees refuse to work with a coworker suspected of having AIDS, what should an employer do?

May employers ask any job applicant if he or she has the disease? No. The handicap and disability laws against discrimination generally prohibit inquiries as to whether an applicant suffers from a handicap or disability. The answer would be irrelevant unless this handicap substantially interferes with the person's ability to do the job being applied for. As a result, under most of these laws, including the ones enacted in New York and Los Angeles, an employer may ask only whether the job applicant suffers from a handicap or a disability that would interfere with job performance. And any inquiry must apply to all applicants, not merely those perceived as "high-risk" for contracting the disease.

An employer may not test workers for AIDS and then fire employees who test positive for the virus. Employees with AIDS cannot be fired unless the illness substantially interferes with their ability to do their jobs or poses a substantial health threat to the work environment. If coworkers refuse to work with an employee suspected of having AIDS, the employer is required to do everything reasonable to accommodate the employee with the disease, including educating other workers and making special arrangements if necessary.

Opposition from fellow employees or clients may make an employer reluctant to keep an AIDS carrier on staff. But where important civil rights are at stake, misunderstanding and uneasiness cannot justify discrimination. Blanket restrictions on employees who are feared to carry the AIDS virus or who have tested positive for it violate employees' legal rights against discrimination. Employers who discriminate may find themselves in losing court battles.

WHAT EMPLOYERS ARE DOING ABOUT IT

America's largest companies have been confronted with the legal problems associated with employment discrimination based on the fear of AIDS. Major corporations such as Citicorp, General Foods, and General Dynamics have developed corporate guidelines on how to deal with the disease. These companies have stated publicly that they do not discriminate against workers with AIDS and have written corporate policies that prohibit such discrimination.

In a survey of 1000 companies nationwide on this subject, the National Gay Rights Advocates, a public-interest law firm, received 164 responses. The study found that a majority of the firms who answered the survey claimed that they did not discriminate against employees with AIDS. The report also showed that nearly all the companies maintained corporate medical plans that covered AIDS-related medical expenses, and only one firm, a pharmaceutical manufacturer, stated that it required employees or job applicants to take medical tests for presence of the disease.

"The survey does not say that discrimination does not exist [or] that all employers are behaving marvelously," said Benjamin Schatz, who directed the survey. "It is still a major problem." Members of the group who sponsored the survey comment that the lack of responses may be very informative. "The large number of firms that did not respond may be telling in itself," said Schatz.

Other businesses have taken the initiative in sponsoring company policies about the disease. Lawyers at Morrison and Foerster's San Francisco law firm have announced a firm AIDS policy. "We felt it better" to develop a policy in advance rather than dealing with it in a crisis mode, Joseph E. Terraciano, managing partner, was quoted as saying in the *National Law Journal* (March 2, 1987). The firm will treat AIDS just like any other life-threatening illness such as cancer, and employees will continue to be eligible for life and health insurance, disability, and leaves of absence. Lawyers in the firm's labor employment group suggested the policy after researching and preparing similar plans for their corporate clients.

Employment discrimination against persons with other STDs is also common and widespread. The recent intensified focus on discrimination against persons with AIDS will lend better legal protection and education to the issue as it concerns all persons who are unfairly terminated from employment.

State laws and court decisions that protect workers with AIDS from losing their jobs will also protect other persons with STDs who are threatened with similar discrimination. Insidious discrimination is generally based on lack of education and fear. Continued court action to protect workers can do a great deal for all persons who have been exposed to an STD and live in fear of unfair discrimination or harassment on the job.

If, however, it could be proved that a particular STD presented a real problem of contagion in the workplace, public health concerns would presumably take precedence over individuals' rights.

Housing Bias

Historically, landlords could refuse to rent to anyone for any reason. As a result, many groups, including minorities, women, and the disabled, were often victims of unfair housing practices. Today, however, federal and state civil rights laws prohibit rental discrimination and can protect the tenant from unfair eviction. These laws can also provide the tenant with a basis for civil action against the landlord that can result in severe financial penalties.

It is illegal for a landlord to refuse to rent leasehold premises on the basis of a group characteristic. (It is legal to discriminate against tenants when the reason is closely related to the landlord's business interest—for example, a poor credit history or poor references.) State law, and in some cases federal law, forbids discrimination on the basis of race, religion, ethnic background, sex, physical disability, or sexual orientation.

In addition, local laws may protect a person against housing discrimination that is not based on a legitimate public health concern. For example, Los Angeles has enacted an ordinance that forbids any kind of discrimination against a person with AIDS. This specifically includes a prohibition against discrimination in housing. If a landlord cannot offer a legitimate basis on which to refuse to rent or on which to base an eviction, the tenant discriminated against can sue the landlord for damages and can win suit charging unlawful eviction.

There have been reports of housing discrimination involving persons with AIDS nationwide. In one case a physician and specialist in internal medicine in Manhattan's Greenwich Village was confronted by a landlord refusing to renew his lease because most of his patients were persons with AIDS. The doctor went to court and won an injunction. Settlement was reached and the doctor was permitted to remain.

Early in this century persons who were infected with communicable diseases that were considered a grave risk to the health of others were subject to state regulation and, in extreme cases, quarantine. These cases involved persons with typhoid, smallpox, or tuberculosis. These situations, however, involved illnesses that medical authorities believed were highly infectious through even casual contact. Health authorities today do not perceive persons with AIDS or most other STDs as posing a substantial health risk to others in their environment.

In spite of that, persons with communicable diseases often encounter discrimination in many areas of their lives. Affected persons can experience such discrimination in health care, employment, public accommodations, and housing. Persons with AIDS in particular are susceptible to it because the disease is often perceived as a health risk to others in the community.

Insurance

Individuals who have been infected with an STD may have difficulty obtaining health insurance. What legal recourse does an individual have against an insurance carrier who refuses to approve an application for health insurance? Can the billion-dollar health insurance industry effectively deny applicants with a history of venereal disease the right to purchase health plans? Is infection with an STD a valid reason for refusal to insure?

The Herpes Resource Center recently devoted its attention to this question in *The Helper,* the newsletter it distributes to members who suffer from genital herpes. The following excerpt describes the health coverage problems that can affect the herpes patient. A similar analysis can be applied to all sexually transmitted diseases. The unique legal problems associated with health and life insurance policies for people with AIDS are addressed in a separate analysis later in this chapter.

The Herpes Resource Center (HRC) printed the following letter from a member who had trouble getting health care coverage.

My case had a happy ending. In a nutshell, I'm writing to relate two things: If someone tries to deny you health care coverage because you have herpes, make noise. If they continue to deny it, make more noise.

First, a little history. My wife (who does not have herpes) and I recently moved from one coast to the other in order to prepare ourselves for new careers. The transition process meant that we needed to obtain our own hospitalization coverage in our new location.

We applied to a local Health Maintenance Organization (HMO) for membership. Shortly after sending our applications, I received a form letter informing me that my membership could not be approved. At the bottom of the page was a blank space and a line that read "Reason(s): Herpes."

I had filled out a health history questionnaire with my application which included a question about herpes. I informed the HMO of my frequent herpes attacks over the past eight years. I average about eight outbreaks a year, though in the fairly stressful circumstances of 1983–1984 the average was more like 10 or 11.

The form letter rejecting my application states: "Based on review of your health statement, you are judged to be an unusual risk to require medical care, the cost of which would be an unfair burden to other members [of the HMO]."

My first reaction was anxiety over my personal predicament, but it was almost instantaneously followed by the realization that the rejection must be fought because it represented an issue with potential impact on 20 million other people with herpes. We're used to being stigmatized for a disease which, when properly handled, is only an annoyance, but could we allow health insurance providers, who should know better, to deny us basic protection with so little cause?

In my particular case, I found the "unusual risk" reason for rejection more than a bit ironic. Since my diagnosis and a follow-up visit more than seven years ago, I had never sought treatment for my herpes. Four years prior to moving I had belonged to an HMO, and my records backed me up. That hardly made . . . my herpes care an "unfair burden" to others.

I was further angered on finding from friends in my new location, who belonged to the HMO that had rejected me, that they had never been specifically asked if they had herpes, apparently because they were members under a group protection plan and therefore were not asked for a detailed health history. I considered that discriminatory.

I left the discrimination issue aside, however, and appealed the decision to reject me via a letter in which I explained my lack of need for medical attention for my herpes. At the end of the letter, I told those making the decision that if they upheld their rejection I would expect a written explanation which addressed, at a minimum, the following questions:

1. Does [the HMO], as a matter of policy, reject all applicants who have genital herpes?

2. If the answer to the first question is no, then why specifically, and in light of the information supplied in my letter, was my application rejected?

Several weeks later, with no explanation for the reversal, I received a confirmation of my acceptance into the health plan. There was no need to carry the battle further.

Though some individuals with herpes may not be as fortunate as I in never needing medical assistance, I think such decisions need to be fought no matter what the circumstances. Herpes is not, in my opinion, a sufficient reason for denying something so basic as medical coverage to anyone. The HRC people, whom I contacted for advice during my battle and who were supportive, agree with me on that.

If any of you are ever denied health coverage due to herpes, here are some things you might consider. First, any denial can be appealed. Write a letter requesting an appeal and provide enough information to back your argument.

I can see several ways to fight a rejection such as mine, if an appeal does not reverse the decision. Fortunately these were not necessary in my case. As a veteran newspaper reporter I am used to working with bureaucracies, and I know how to make one react. For those of you who aren't that fortunate, some advice:

- Use the HRC for advice and support. The staff there, who you support by your membership, were ready to throw their considerable knowledge and influence in these matters into the fray on my behalf if the need had arisen.
- Bring your message to the public via the local media. People with herpes are everywhere, and if an issue such as this doesn't touch a nerve with them, it's hard to envision one that would.
- Consider seeking help. A class action suit on behalf of individuals with herpes, and maybe a discrimination or personal damage suit on your own behalf, would get results. Check with the HRC, the American Civil Liberties Union, and any consumer groups you belong to for possible material assistance if you can't afford it yourself. Stress the larger public ramifications of such exclusions as a means of attracting their support.
- Consider political pressure. Find out who licenses the HMO or insurance plan that's rejecting you and seek ways to have their insurance licenses suspended or revoked if they won't change their minds. You can make the case that, based on the relative innocuousness of herpes as a health threat, the rejecting agency is hardly fulfilling a mandate to serve the public by denying coverage to the 20% of the public that has herpes. You may need, again, the clout of larger groups such as the HRC to move bureaucrats (or the politicians who can move them) into action.

One final word: Be prepared to publicly admit you have herpes. The doctors in my previous HMO and others I sought advice from felt that people with herpes may be especially vulnerable to such actions because they are afraid to attract attention to themselves and their disease by fighting. That's not hard to understand, given that, in my case, even medical professionals were willing to stigmatize me for having herpes, but you should try not to let it deter you.

Whatever else, don't get discouraged. No one needs the kind of potentially time-consuming challenge presented by such a dilemma, but if you are presented with such a challenge, grit your teeth and stick to your guns. In my case I did not have a difficult task—a letter of appeal was sufficient—but if you do please try to bear in mind that you may be helping a lot more people than yourself by pursuing what's right and succeeding.

ADVICE ABOUT INSURANCE

Any individual who is rejected by a health insurer because of medical history has a right to appeal the company's decision if that person feels that his or her history has been misinterpreted. A letter of appeal, in some cases, may be enough. It worked for the herpes sufferer who wrote to the HRC. His experience illustrates the importance of fighting unfair decisions. The person who has been discriminated against because he has an STD must challenge that decision. It may not be easy and it may require engaging professional legal assistance to get results. Individual effort can add up to collective change.

For your own protection, never conceal medical history or lie about it on your application for health insurance. Misrepresentation can give an insurance company valid grounds to contest the policy and refuse payment. Basic contract law provides that if coverage is issued to the insured on the basis of misrepresentation, the contract is voidable at the option of the insurance company. There are statutes in most states, however, that prohibit the contestability of a policy after a certain amount of time has elapsed—often the period is two years for most policies.

Is venereal disease sufficient grounds for an insurance carrier to turn down an application for health insurance? Most insurance company executives will answer no. But the fact is that venereal disease has been an important factor in rejecting health coverage applicants.

SPECIAL CONSIDERATIONS: AIDS AND INSURANCE DISCRIMINATION

The increasing concern over AIDS has had a dramatic impact on the insurance industry. Faced with a growing number of AIDS-related claims by policyholders, insurance companies are rewriting corporate guidelines regarding acceptance of applications for insurance and are cautioning agents about accepting applicants with "immoral lifestyles" or a medical history of venereal disease.

Can an insurance company refuse to insure an applicant because he is male and single or because he lives in a neighborhood with a large homosexual population? Can it refuse to sell him a life insurance policy if the listed beneficiary is not a wife or child or if he has previously been infected with a reportable venereal disease?

Dr. Robert Gleeson, an expert on AIDS with Northwest Mutual Life Insurance, stated on *Nightline* that his company does not use facts about lifestyle, geography, or sexual orientation in its underwriting process. (Underwriting involves the decision process by which an insurance company determines the acceptability of risk and agrees to assume it in return for the payment of premiums.) Dr. Gleeson comments, however, that Northwest will use the results of a blood test for any person applying for insurance who is above a certain age or desires a certain policy amount. On the basis of the results of that blood test, Dr. Gleeson admits, an applicant can be rejected or accepted.

Another company, Munich American Reassurance, of Atlanta, has taken more drastic action. It has issued a set of specific directives telling underwriters to watch for applicants with admitted histories of STDs or intravenous drug use. The measures urge underwriters to treat single marital status, residence in areas with high concentrations of AIDS cases, or the naming of a roommate or friend as the beneficiary of the policy as "potentially indicative" of an increased risk of exposure to AIDS.

Other insurance companies, too, are rumored to use various screening techniques to weed out high-risk applicants, although most of these companies deny discrimination.

Such measures have outraged legal advocacy groups. Gay activists complain that the new guidelines constitute "lifestyle screening" that discriminates against homosexual males. Legal and medical experts are also expressing concern that the new underwriting policies are far too broad and discriminatory. Others feel that the measures may contribute to the spread of the AIDS virus by causing some individuals with the disease to go underground. When a person fears that he may be rejected for insurance on the grounds that he has had a history of one or more sexually transmitted diseases, he may try to hide the information from doctors or public health agencies.

California has enacted state laws against the use of HTLV-III (now usually called HIV) blood tests for the purposes of acceptance or rejection of an applicant for insurance. The California law, enacted in 1985, provides that "the results of a blood test to detect antibodies to the probable causative agent [of AIDS] ... shall not be used in any instance for the determination of insurability or suitability for employment."

A law adopted by the District of Columbia in 1986 provides for the same protections and further prohibits the use of classification factors such as age, sex, marital status, place of residence, or sexual orientation in determining either individuals who will be offered insurance coverage or premium rates.

In states where screening is against the law, insurance companies like California's Transamerica have circumvented the law by administering a different test. Transamerica now requires a special immune system blood test from applicants who seek high-face-value policies and/or live in areas the CDC says have high numbers of AIDS cases. Unlike the forbidden HIV test, the screening method used by Transamerica, the "T-cell test," does not test specifically for AIDS but indicates a possible immune system breakdown that could be caused by a variety of medical reasons.

In states where the test is not specifically prohibited by law, large numbers of insurance companies have begun including the "enzyme-linked immunosorbent assay" (ELISA) blood test, which detects the antibody to the AIDS virus in human serum and plasma, in their medical examinations of insurance applicants. A positive test result will lead to the rejection of the applicant's policy.

Antibody testing by insurance companies raises important issues concerning informed consent and confidentiality. Disclosure of test results can have dramatic effects on an individual's personal and professional life, and test results obtained by the insurance carrier should remain strictly confidential. In at least one case a plaintiff has received a financial settlement against a major insurance company after the applicant alleged he was tested without his consent and the insurance carrier failed to guard the confidentiality of the test results.

What is the responsibility of insurance carriers as the holders and transmitters of information? What is an insurance company's responsibility with regard to interpretation of test results and counseling? Under what circumstances can insurance carriers reveal test results to third parties? Should providing test results to co-operative information services, like the Medical Information Bureau, be allowed, making the test information available to queries from other insurance companies, even those in states where the test is prohibited? A number of these issues remain unsettled.

The strong reaction to the AIDS problem by the insurance industry and the scrutiny of applicants in the search for those who are at risk for developing AIDS may affect all persons who have had any sexually transmitted disease. Applicants who have been infected with venereal disease at any point in their lives may find themselves unable to purchase health and life insurance, especially since studies have indicated that persons who have had a venereal disease are at a higher risk for contracting the AIDS virus. A recent study published by the Venereal Disease Association journal, *Sexually Transmitted Diseases,* reports that in a group of 87 homosexual AIDS patients, 85 percent had a prior history of gonorrhea and 60 percent had previously had syphilis. Insurance companies use these statistics to create classification schemes to reduce the number of applicants who are at high risk for contracting AIDS.

As a result, individuals who have had venereal disease may be denied health coverage, especially in the private sector. Most state laws do not require insurance companies to insure everyone. And when the insurance industry recognizes increased risk to applicants who have had STDs, denial of insurance applications is likely to occur.

What does it all mean? Insurance companies can screen applicants through use of the HIV tests where not forbidden by state law. Classification schemes, however, that are based on criteria like sexual orientation that are overly broad or underinclusive may violate state unfair-trade-practice laws. These laws provide that discrimination between similarly situated persons with respect to rates, policies, or benefits constitutes an unfair trade practice. Unfair discrimination is the focus.

Lawsuits now pending in U.S. courts will challenge the classification schemes developed by the insurance industry and determine if in fact they constitute unfair discrimination in violation of trade practice laws. At stake is the underlying issue of who should be responsible for the cost of AIDS health care and who should be permitted or denied the opportunity to purchase insurance.

Limited sources of coverage may be available to the person with AIDS or another STD who is denied health insurance coverage. Thirteen states administer shared-risk insurance pools into which all insurers contribute. Residents of these states who have been denied insurance in the private sector qualify, but they must pay increased premiums—often as much as 150 percent more than average rates.

One insurance company in Santa Monica, California, received approval from the Department of Insurance to sell medical insurance policies for acquired immune deficiency syndrome. The company's brochure advertises "AIDS medical expense insurance that pays up to $78,000 per year" for an annual premium of $291. In Dallas another insurance company offered a similar policy but discontinued the program because of poor demand. "AIDS insurance policies" like the one described here generally have limited coverage and expensive premiums. The policy does not cover general health requirements, only those related to the AIDS virus. These policies are best viewed as a supplement to another, fully comprehensive health care plan.

For those who already have insurance coverage, it is important that the insured be aware of their legal rights in this area and make sure that their coverage is maintained. Insurance coverage for AIDS, genital herpes, or any other venereal disease depends on the term of the policy, state insurance laws, and representations made at the time the policy was purchased.

All of these factors must be investigated because any one of them may give the insured the right to continued coverage despite an insurance company's attempt to rescind or deny the policy.

Although insurance policies will differ, they consistently contain certain uniform provisions that are important to the problems of enforcing insurance coverage. Let's examine some of these provisions.

Incontestability provisions.   State laws and insurance policies often contain rules that prohibit the company from denying benefits after a certain period of time because of misrepresentations made by an insured on the policy application. In general, this period of time is two years. After the two years have elapsed, the carrier cannot deny benefits of the policy. This provision is particularly important because carriers are increasingly denying benefits and coverage to persons with AIDS, claiming that the insured misrepresented his medical health to the insurance company when he bought the policy.

Preexisting condition.   Some carriers might claim that AIDS or infection with an STD is a preexisting condition and cancel the policy. And a preexisting condition often forms the basis for a company's denial of coverage. In order for a condition to be considered preexisting, symptoms must have clearly manifested themselves before the policy goes into effect.

One lawsuit against a California insurance carrier that refused to make good on its policy has already reached settlement. William Horner, a 32-year-old man with AIDS, won reinstatement of his health coverage and an undisclosed financial payment from Great Republic Life Insurance when he challenged the company's unlawful denial of policy benefits.

Horner brought the suit when the company refused to cover his medical costs, claiming his illness was a preexisting condition. According to court records, the policy went into effect June 1, but his condition was not diagnosed until June 17. The plaintiff's attorney, Alice Philipson, stated in *AIDS Policy and Law* (December 1986) that the settlement "sends a strong message to insurers that they will not be able to use the pre-existing condition clause" to refuse payment for AIDS. Unfortunately, William Horner died two weeks after the settlement was reached. The decision sets an important precedent for similar litigation now pending.

Notice conditions.   This may assist individuals whose premiums may not have been paid or where coverage has recently lapsed. Notice requirements are written in the policy and are part of state law. If the notice process is not faithfully followed by a carrier, the policy in some cases may be renewed retroactive to the date of improper termination.

Sexual orientation.   State insurance regulators have now adopted guidelines preventing companies from using a person's "sexual orientation" to determine if life or health insurance policies should be issued. These model guidelines bar carriers from using marital status, living arrangements, occupation, gender, or geographic location to establish a person's sexual orientation. Failure to follow these guidelines may constitute violation of state insurance regulation law and illegal discrimination.

Persons seeking insurance must make every effort to uphold

their legal rights in this area. Persons who are already insured must be aware of their legal right to enforce maintenance of a policy. Where a carrier is unresponsive to such challenges, individuals should hire private counsel or contact public advocacy groups to assert their legal rights.

Children and Public Schools

Children too face STD-related discrimination, especially where AIDS and herpes are involved. The admission of STD-linked children into public school classrooms has often set off community hysteria. Angry parents have withdrawn their children from school, and others have threatened court action. In some cities school boycotts and protests have lasted for months.

Here are some of the latest headlines:

- In Council Bluffs, Iowa, a kindergarten child with herpes set off a wave of community hysteria that included school boycotts and outcries from angry parents. The local education association sought a preliminary injunction against the admission of the child to public school, and after a two-day hearing, Judge Donald O'Brien issued a decision allowing the child to go to school on the condition that the child be examined every morning by her mother for visible lesions and driven to school by the family.

  Before mingling with other children, the child was ordered to be examined by the school nurse. If lesions were found to exist, the child was sent home until they were healed. All this was to be done, according to statements made by the court, "as discreetly as possible and without any fanfare."

- An Orange County, California, boy who tested positive for the AIDS antibody was permitted to return to the classroom after heated courtroom debate. The 11-year-old fifth grader, who is a hemophiliac, was exposed to the disease through transfusions of a blood clotting agent. Attorneys for the child claim the decision is a "victory," upholding state law that permits suspension of children only where they pose a contagion danger to other students.

- In Maryland teachers were so worried about becoming infected by elementary school students with herpes that they demanded a lifetime job guarantee for teachers infected in the line of duty and indemnification for teachers sued because of classroom transmission. The demands were triggered by the enrollment of a 6-year-old first grader who had the herpes virus. The teachers' demands were never met.

- In New York City three children were removed from classrooms by school board superintendents who suspected that the students' mother's boyfriend was infected with AIDS.

- A 4-year-old child with AIDS was barred from the classroom in Washington Borough, New Jersey, along with her healthy 9-year-old brother. Parents of healthy students have organized legal action against the child and her family.

What is the uproar about? Do children with STDs pose a serious health threat to other children? It has been shown that in most cases they do not. What causes parents and teachers to react so violently over the admission of STD-linked children? Clearly, it is fear, most often irrational and caused by lack of the proper information.

Should STD-linked Children Be Allowed to Attend School?

The answer is yes as long as the medical condition of the child does not threaten the health of other children in the classroom. Infected children can be prevented from attending public school only if authorities have medical evidence that their infection poses a serious health threat to other children. The health hazard must be established by scientific evidence and not be based on irrational fear or public sentiment.

HOW CAN WE PROTECT CHILDREN
FROM DISCRIMINATION IN SCHOOL?

Children are protected by federal laws that enable them to obtain education in the public school system without discrimination. These laws prohibit discrimination against any disabled schoolchildren on the basis of physical handicaps or perceived handicaps. These federal statutes include the Rehabilitation Act of 1973 [29 U.S.C. Sec. 701] and the Education of the Handicapped Act (20 U.S.C. Sec. 1400–1454). The latter statute is also known as the Education for All Handicapped Children Act. Schoolchildren are also protected against discrimination under the equal protection clause of the Fourteenth Amendment. But despite federal protection, many children with STDs have received nationwide attention when they exercise their right to attend public school.

Herpes and AIDS are the two diseases that cause the most violent outbursts among adults.

As for herpes in children, the medical consensus is that this is neither a serious problem, a new problem, nor a preventable problem. In each of the explosive school situations that have made headlines, the medical opinion was that the problem rested on misinformation and overreaction to the word *herpes* rather than any real threat in the school. AIDS, however, cannot be dealt with so easily, not necessarily because of the real threat it presents but because of the terror it engenders.

CHILDREN WITH AIDS

How Do Children Get AIDS?

Infants can become infected in utero by a mother infected with the AIDS virus. Children can become infected with AIDS through transfusions of blood or blood products.

The kind of discrimination faced by schoolchildren with AIDS is dramatically illustrated by the case of three young boys in Arcadia, Florida. The three brothers, aged 8, 9, and 10, are hemophiliacs. Each of the brothers has tested positive for the AIDS antibody. Each was exposed to the disease through HIV-contaminated blood product transfusions.

When the family confided in their local clergyman about the boys' condition, Baptist Minister Raul Gamiloten responded by spreading the news throughout the congregation and barring the family from his church services. "Anyone who says [he is] not afraid of AIDS is a fool or a liar," Gamiloten preached.

Even though local authorities have stated that the boys pose little danger to others in the community of Arcadia, the local school board has not allowed the children to attend public school. The children have been denied participation in the town's annual fishing tournament, and the town's barbershop has refused to cut their hair.

The father of the boys, Cliff Ray, is saddened by the town's treatment of his sons. Someday, he said, the town will realize that they "treated these young 'uns very wrong."

The Rays' federal lawsuit demanding that the children be given a public education prompted community reprisals, including the burning down of the Ray home. The family has moved to another (they hope more understanding) area.

When Ricky, aged 10, was asked what he would like to do more than anything, he said, "Go to school, so I can play with other kids and get a good job when I grow up."

The Ray brothers illustrate the deplorable discrimination suffered by school-age children because of AIDS-related fears.

Should Children with AIDS Be Permitted in School?

In June 1987 there were 504 cases of children with AIDS, according to the Centers for Disease Control; 322 have already died. It is also estimated that between 1987 and 1991 some 4000 babies will contract the disease before birth.

Children who test HIV-positive face enormous social stigmas and discrimination. The parents of healthy children have widely protested the presence of children with AIDS in the public schools. As a result of the controversy, the American Academy of Pediatrics has advanced the following recommendations:

- Most children with AIDS should be allowed to attend school, with the approval of their physician.
- Children with AIDS who have lack of control of their body secretions, have a tendency to bite others, or have open sores should be placed in more restrictive school settings.
- Screening of all schoolchildren for AIDS is unnecessary and should not be undertaken.

The National Education Association (NEA) has asserted that "children with AIDS should not be barred from classes without review by panels that include the child's parents, health experts, and school officials." If there is reasonable cause, the recommendation states, to believe that a student or an employee might be infected with AIDS, the school should be able to require that person to undergo a medical evaluation.

It is likely that many courts will follow these guidelines. In New York, after an emotional and costly five-week court battle characterized by "distress and acrimony," the court confirmed New York's case-by-case decision-making policy regarding children with AIDS. The court ruled that the policy not to exclude schoolchildren with the disease automatically had a rational basis and that automatic exclusion would be a violation of the Vocational Rehabilitation Act of 1973 and the equal protection clause of the Fourteenth Amendment. Similar cases are pending in many states.

Another New York case, this one involving the segregation of students who were infected with hepatitis B, serves as an excellent analogy to cases involving students who are AIDS victims. In this case the court held that the segregation of students with hepatitis B from healthy students violated federal laws against discrimination against the handicapped.

Like AIDS, hepatitis B has no known cure and can be transmitted through sexual contact, exposure to contaminated blood, or in utero infection. The Centers for Disease Control stated that the transmission of hepatitis B approximates the worst-case scenario for the spread of AIDS, because the risk of acquiring hepatitis B is "far in excess" of the risks of contracting the AIDS virus. It is against the law to exclude children with hepatitis from public school. By analogy, it may also be illegal to discriminate against children with genital herpes or AIDS.

The case presents an excellent model for analysis of the issues involving children with AIDS or other STDs. In most situations, barring a serious and real health threat to other children, it is a denial of basic civil rights to prevent students with AIDS or genital herpes from attending public school.

To bolster evidence that the disease poses little threat in casual settings, the CDC reports that there have been no cases of children who have contracted the disease in a public school or day-care center. The CDC has issued its own report on the topic, recommending, like other groups of experts, that schools restrict only AIDS-infected children who lack control of body secretions, are prone to biting other children, or have exposed or open lesions.

Even the most rational parents may feel uneasy knowing their children are associating in a school setting with children who are carriers of the AIDS virus. But it is the real threat of medical contagion and not the perceived threat by the public that courts must consider in determining the public school cases. The worry of parents with school-age children is understandable. Yet even in this emotion-charged context the Constitution requires that courts ground their decisions in reality and allow AIDS children to attend public school when they present no risk to other students.

8

AIDS and Legal Controversy

All STDs leave their imprint on the human psyche, but none have the impact of the deadly AIDS virus. Even the so-called low-risk or no-risk groups have reacted with a fear often bordering on panic.

The appearance of AIDS in our midst has had some very complex legal implications. It is imperative for everyone in any way connected with the disease—patients, their lovers, those in fear of being infected, those who care for them medically and otherwise—to be aware of these legal implications.

Liability for Sexual Transmission of AIDS

The primary means of contracting the AIDS virus is sexual contact. The best protection is to refrain from sex with infected persons or persons whose health history is unknown. In the alternative, safe sex practices, including the use of a latex condom to reduce the likelihood of transmission, are a good idea.

The following sexual practices are believed to pose the greatest risk of infection with the AIDS virus:

- Anal intercourse with intraanal ejaculation by an infected partner

- Vaginal intercourse with internal ejaculation by an infected partner
- Oral ingestion of an infected partner's ejaculate

When one person infects another with the AIDS virus, an injury with lifetime consequences has occurred. If a partner is completely unaware that he has the virus, no legal liability will attach. If a person suspects that he might have symptoms of the disease or has engaged in high-risk behavior, he must disclose this to any sexual partner and must take reasonable steps to prevent transmission both to protect his lover from the AIDS virus and to protect himself from potential legal liability.

If a person is aware of his infection, he owes each and every sexual partner a mandatory duty of full disclosure. Where one party offers false assurances that he or she is free from infection, that partner can face serious civil liability.

In fact, as an article in the New York ·Times (June 19, 1987) stated:

> The cases now in the justice system have already raised legal questions about whether the HIV virus can be treated as a deadly weapon under law, and whether people who knowingly transmit it can and should be . . . prosecuted for assault or attempted murder.

Thus false statements and deliberate transmission can lead to criminal action as well.

As with the other STDs described in this book, failure to make full disclosure about a relevant medical condition that affects the health and well-being of a sexual partner is grounds for tort action. The grounds and all other legal points are generally the same as those for all STDs; these are discussed elsewhere in this book. The differences are presented here.

CAUSATION CONSIDERATIONS

Because of the incubation period for the HIV virus (currently estimated to be up to eight years) proof of the source of infection in an AIDS-related STD case can be very difficult. Since the virus can lay dormant for years, a person could be infected over a long period of time without knowing it, complicating the task of pinpointing the date and source of infection. Plaintiffs who have engaged in sexual activity with multiple partners may find it very difficult to determine the actual transmitter, especially if several of these partners could be considered "high risk."

However, the source of infection is a factual question that is decided by the jury according to the weight of the evidence. And where a plaintiff can prove by a preponderance of the evidence that the defendant had the virus and transmitted it to the plaintiff, liability will be fixed. Clearly, in an HIV-related case, establishing causation in the majority of cases would be difficult, if not impossible. Even when the hurdles of causation can be met, other problems remain. HIV cases may be more subject to defenses of contributory negligence or assumption of risk, and damages in certain cases would be speculative.

DAMAGES

The injury to a plaintiff is far more serious than damages for other sexually transmitted diseases, and the issues of harm and damages may require new legal interpretation. Even if the plaintiff does not die from the infection, actual damages can be enormous because of staggering medical costs.

There has been a wide range of medical cost estimates. Although a Rand Corporation study claims the cost of treatment can be as much as $150,000 per patient, San Francisco hospital costs have been reported as $60,000 to $75,000 per patient, with some as low as $28,000. A defendant who is found liable for the transmission of AIDS may be expected to offset these costs. In addition to damages based on medical expenses, a plaintiff could obtain compensation for lost wages, pain and suffering, and support services.

Further, if the infection was intentional and willful, punitive damages may be appropriate. In assessing a punitive award a jury would take into consideration not only the catastrophic impact this disease can cause, but wealth of the defendant as well.

Proof of damages is especially problematic in lawsuits brought by asymptomatic plaintiffs seeking compensation for emotional trauma. Courts generally will not allow recovery for pain and suffering without some tangible injury and it is uncertain whether mere exposure to HIV without the development of symptoms is sufficient injury on which to base monetary recovery.

If the plaintiff dies as a result of the infection, the plaintiff's estate could institute legal proceedings if none had previously been filed. Theoretically, such an action could be brought under the state's wrongful death or survival statutes, subject to the court's interpretation. The plaintiff's estate could maintain an action against the defendant for transmitting the disease. In the event that the defendant has died, the plaintiff can sue his estate, as Rock Hudson's lover is doing. However, there may be few instances in which the estate has not been depleted by medical expenses. The value of a lawsuit for damages may be valid in only a small minority of cases.

STATUTE OF LIMITATIONS

A plaintiff must file suit within the period of time prescribed by the statute of limitations in his state, and this differs from state to state. As explained earlier, an action must be filed within a specified period from the date of the infection or, in some states, the date of knowledge of injury. Because of the potential latency period between becoming infected with HIV and the appearance of symptoms, persons with AIDS may have enormous difficulty in meeting statute deadlines for filing civil actions.

Even a diligent plaintiff who submits to testing on a regular basis may carry the virus but not be susceptible to diagnosis. In a different situation, a victim who is diagnosed as a carrier of the virus may not develop AIDS for several years—if he ever does—and not suffer physical harm on which to base legal action. This may force a plaintiff in this context to bring legal action before any compensable or reasonably measured harm has occurred. The statute of limitations may prove to be unforgiving to the plaintiff in AIDS-related litigation.

MANDATORY DUTY OF DISCLOSURE

Persons with AIDS, like persons with any STD, are duty bound to make full and complete disclosure of health history and sexual history to every sexual partner. Persons who have tested positive for HIV but have not developed symptoms have the same obligation. Failure to do so can result in legal liability and stiff dollar damages. Every person owes it to his or her sexual partner to engage in safer sex, based on respect for each other's health and well-being, as well as a healthy respect for the law.

AIDS-Related Malpractice

In southern Florida in one year, seven people committed suicide after they were told they had tested positive for the AIDS virus. These tragic and unnecessary suicides indicate the importance of proper medical counseling by physicians regarding the HIV test. A positive test result does not necessarily mean the person tested will develop the disease. Patients should be informed that the test is designed only to detect antibodies, showing exposure to HIV, and that the test does not indicate whether a person will develop AIDS in the future or will remain healthy. Failure by a physician to provide full information about the nature of the test and the meaning of the test results could give rise to a lawsuit in negligence. This happened in one of these suicide cases: The victim's family is now considering a wrongful death action against the doctor and hospital who negligently failed to inform their 28-year-old son about the proper interpretation of the test results.

The point of this section is not to encourage AIDS patients into litigation against physicians who work very hard to care for patients with the disease but to make patients aware of the standard of care that a doctor owes them so that they will insist on receiving that care. Lawsuits can be avoided, and the patient-doctor relationship will be improved.

DIAGNOSIS

The physician treating a patient with AIDS is faced with unique and difficult challenges. Problems related to the diagnosis of the disease may give rise to lawsuits for medical malpractice against the physician. These potential causes of action can be based on a failure to diagnose AIDS, an erroneous diagnosis, a failure to inform a patient properly of the diagnosis, or a failure to provide proper counseling related to an HIV antibody test. An AIDS patient who was wrongly diagnosed, an infant whose parents were misdiagnosed, or persons who have been infected by an AIDS patient who was wrongly diagnosed all have the right of legal recovery.

Untimely or Erroneous Diagnosis

Diagnostic testing provides physicians with clinical information that may or may not lead to the need for additional patient testing. If additional testing is not ordered when the circumstances dictate it, this may constitute medical malpractice. A doctor who suspects that a patient may have been exposed to the AIDS virus must inform that patient of the need for proper HIV blood testing. This is available in clinics that offer AIDS testing and counseling. Failure to do so can result in physician liability.

The potential liability of a physician for untimely diagnosis is measured by the amount of damage that misdiagnosis has caused. An AIDS patient may die from the disease in a relatively short period of time; an untimely diagnosis may have aggravated the patient's condition. If a delayed diagnosis causes a patient's condition to get worse and, as a result, shortens the patient's life, such a delay causes damage for which a patient can recover in a court of law.

Many court cases involving physician delay in the diagnosis of cancer have been successfully fought by plaintiffs or by their successors following their untimely deaths. The cases are analogous here. The failure to diagnose a physical condition such as AIDS can cause a delay in obtaining treatment. For example, if a patient whose AIDS infection is diagnosed early comes down with *Pneumocystis carinii* pneumonia, an opportunistic infection, a physician can refer the patient for treatment with the drug Retrovir, which, in some cases, seems to slow the progression of the disease. The medication is now widely available from the Burroughs Wellcome Company.

According to research by the Institute of Medicine of the National Academy of Sciences, with early physician diagnosis and treatment with drug therapy, 90 percent of AIDS patients with *Pneumocystis carinii* pneumonia can survive the first episode of the disease.

A timely and accurate medical diagnosis can also provide the AIDS sufferer with another important benefit. It can enable the patient to take appropriate measures to reduce his exposure to other infections that might further damage the immune system. As treatment techniques improve in the near future, they will likely be directed at combating the disease early in its development. This increases the importance of early and accurate medical diagnosis and increases the physician's liability if he fails to meet this standard of care.

Along the same lines of reasoning, any treatment to be developed in the future for AIDS will require intervention early in the progression of the disease. A misdiagnosis can delay application of new medical discoveries. The harm the patient suffers in these cases would be the lost chance to recuperate from the underlying disease. Some jurisdictions do not permit recovery in lawsuits for such a lost chance of recovery, but most courts are increasingly recognizing such claims as actionable losses for damages.

A complete failure to diagnose a patient's condition as AIDS may give rise to a cause of action for negligent infliction of emotional distress. This claim would be based on the severe anxiety and distress caused by a wrong diagnosis that delayed needed treatment for the disease.

Incorrect Positive Diagnosis

If a patient is told that he has tested positive for the disease when that is not the case, the incorrect diagnosis can constitute grounds for legal action in tort. The legal theory would be based on the negligent infliction of emotional distress. An incorrect positive diagnosis without at least proper counseling could result in catastrophic and disabling emotional anxiety and depression.

Psychologists are now reporting responses of "AIDS anxiety" among gay men who are asymptomatic carriers of the AIDS virus. These are men who test positive for the antibody but have no discernible symptoms of the disease. Many of these men have exhibited common emotional side effects that have been described by psychiatrists and psychologists studying the problem. In some cases the anxiety can be so severe that it causes the asymptomatic person to become completely unable to cope with day-to-day living.

This phenomenon was described by Morin in "The Psychological Impact of AIDS on Gay Men" in *American Psychologist* (1984) magazine:

> Since the onset of AIDS in the gay community some asymptomatic gay men have begun to manifest acute psychological symptoms that include panic attacks, generalized anxiety, and persistent hypochondrias characterized by somatic reactions that mimic AIDS symptoms such as night sweats and fatigue. . . . Many cases of AIDS-related anxiety states are so severe as to cause impairment in social and occupational functioning. Obsessive thought and fears about AIDS intrude on people at inopportune moments, causing problems in concentration on the job or at home. Panic attacks sometimes result in poor occupation performance, loss of work time, strained friendships and primary partner relationships, and repeated visits to emergency rooms, AIDS screening clinics, and the offices of mental health professionals.

People who think they have been infected with HIV because of a doctor's misdiagnosis can exhibit similar psychological symptoms, and the responsible physician may be liable. Damages would be measured by the emotional impact on the patient and could include medical costs for psychological therapy and counseling. If the patient has also lost his job due to AIDS anxiety, the treating doctor may also be liable for lost wages to the extent that the psychological distress impaired the plaintiff's ability to work.

In some jurisdictions recovery based on psychic injury without physical harm is not permitted. However, a showing of gross negligence on the part of the physician may facilitate a plaintiff's court action. Gross negligence could theoretically be established if a doctor failed to counsel the patient properly or failed to reconfirm test results, given the acute consequences of shock and anxiety that could result from an incorrect diagnosis.

FAILURE TO INFORM

Failure to inform a patient that he has the disease is grounds for action against the physician. It prevents early treatment of the disease and in some cases may prevent treatment altogether. It is highly unlikely that a physician would fail to inform a person if his test results were positive. In situations, however, where the test is administered for ancillary purposes, like employment, insurance, or blood donor screening, the issue is significantly different. In such situations it is unclear whether a physician-patient relationship exists that places on the doctor the duty to warn the patient of the results and the interpretation of those results.

When tests are administered privately, the doctor *must* inform the patient. Failure to do so can result in physician liability based on the patient's inability to obtain timely treatment.

Physicians disagree on whether prospective blood donors should be told about their test results. Some fear that persons would offer to donate blood to get a free test and skew the present system for blood donor screening. Other officials feel strongly that after the testing of blood for any purpose, the results should be given to the person tested, combined with proper counseling.

PHYSICIAN CONFIDENTIALITY

Although some states have laws governing the confidentiality of medical information, there are no federal guidelines regarding the distribution of test results, and there are cases where results have been sent in the mail or accidentally reported over the phone to unsuspecting family members. In one case a woman was notified accidentally that her husband's HIV test results were positive. She had had no idea that her husband was even tested. Such behavior would be actionable in states that have appropriate laws.

Physicians must safeguard the confidentiality of a patient's medical condition. Disclosure of test results involves important ethical and legal considerations. Disclosure of a positive diagnosis could invite such dire effects as loss of employment, eviction, and acts of discrimination.

In addition to the duty physicians have to their patients, the law also recognizes, in certain situations, a duty to third persons. A number of cases have asserted an obligation incumbent on physicians or therapists to warn third persons where there is a likelihood of violent behavior and the identity of the intended victim is known to the physician or therapist. At present these conflicting obligations are unsettled.

Similar concerns surround the issue of contact tracing, where public health officials trace sex partners of persons with AIDS. This form of investigation raises serious questions about an individual's right to privacy and the public health.

INFORMED CONSENT

In addition, a doctor should never administer the test without the full and informed consent of the test taker. The patient cannot give full and informed consent unless he understands the nature of the test and its significance. A doctor can face further liability in tort damages where results are obtained without consent and then later used for the purpose of employment or insurance discrimination.

PHYSICIAN LIABILITY

Wrongful Birth

As mentioned earlier, the Centers for Disease Control estimate that by 1991 some 4000 babies will have contracted AIDS while in the womb. If a physician has failed to diagnose AIDS or to inform parents that an unborn child might be infected with AIDS as a result of the disease in time for a mother to terminate the pregnancy, this can result in legal liability. Courts increasingly recognize a cause of action for wrongful birth based on a doctor's negligence.

The CDC has recommended that women who test positive for the HIV antibody and who are pregnant or likely to become pregnant should be counseled so that they can make informed choices. Such counseling is intended to permit a woman to choose to delay pregnancy until more is known about prenatal transmission.

The CDC has suggested that women who show evidence of HIV infection, women who use intravenous drugs, women who engage in prostitution, or women who have sexual partners in high-risk groups should be told about the HIV test, tested, and given counseling.

What damages are permitted in an action for wrongful birth? Parents can seek medical and other expenses required to raise the child. In some instances parents have been granted recovery for pecuniary losses attributable to the physician's failure to inform parents of the risk and damages for their own emotional distress. In wrongful birth cases, damages are not sought on behalf of the child but are recovered by the parents.

Physicians must inform women at risk about the possibilities of harm to an infant connected with the disease. Failure to do so when appropriate can result in charges of negligence.

Refusal to Treat

Discrimination by health care workers against persons with AIDS is widespread. Refusal by medical professionals to treat patients sounds inconceivable, but instances of such discrimination have been reported throughout the nation. In Texas dentists have openly refused to treat AIDS sufferers. Ambulance companies in Los Angeles and San Francisco have refused to transport persons with AIDS. In New York patients with AIDS may wait

Other dental workers have been infected by the virus, but they apparently had been members of high-risk groups for the disease. The New York City dentist had practiced dentistry for over 14 years and admitted that he did not wear gloves consistently. The dentist and his wife denied that they were members of any other risk group and claimed to have had no other sex partners.

These studies demonstrate a clear risk to health workers who do not strictly follow CDC guidelines for preventing exposure, and perhaps some even to those who do follow the guidelines. Dr. Anthony Fauci of the National Institutes of Health, a major authority on AIDS, states that there is a "finite risk" associated with health care workers who care for patients with the disease. Dr. Fauci reported to a nationwide audience during ABC-TV's "National Town Meeting on AIDS" that the risk is less than a fraction of 1 percent. "The risk," he said, "is real, but very, very small." Workers who were infected, Dr. Fauci agreed, did not follow important precautionary procedures.

TRANSMISSION OF AIDS TO HEALTH CARE WORKERS

Medical studies have reported that HIV has been detected in most body fluids of people who have the virus. These include blood, saliva, urine, breast milk, tears, spinal fluid, vaginal and cervical secretions, and bone marrow. However, other studies have suggested that it is unlikely that the virus can be transmitted by saliva or tears. Semen and blood remain the most effective transmitters.

AIDS can be spread when infected body fluids come into contact with skin that is cut, has open lesions, or is severely chapped. This fact appears to expose health workers to some risk. After careful study the Centers for Disease Control found only a handful of cases involving health worker contamination, and these workers apparently failed to exercise the necessary precautions. The CDC monitored workers who had direct exposure to infected blood through needle pricks, cuts with contaminated instruments, and exposure to mucous membranes and open skin lesions. The CDC has concluded that the risk is very small when proper guidelines are followed.

The guidelines are generally the same as health care providers are expected to follow with patients who are infected with hepatitis B. These recommendations include special care to avoid needle pricks and scalpel injuries and the wearing of protective clothing, such as gloves, gowns, masks, and goggles, when appropriate.

During invasive procedures, health officials have suggested additional precautions. These include "barrier precautions" like face masks, eye coverings, and waterproof gowns. Physicians and workers with lesions or weeping dermatitis are precluded from performing surgery or other invasive procedures on AIDS patients.

In 1987, the CDC issued stronger guidelines. These recommendations emphasize its position that health care workers should treat all patients as being potentially infected with HIV or other blood-borne diseases and "adhere rigorously" to infection control precautions. Use of these "universal precautions" for handling blood and other body fluids should minimize the risk to health care workers.

These guidelines also address procedures that should be adopted by dentists, mandating that all dentists should consider blood, saliva, and gingival fluid from patients to be potentially infectious and urging the use of gloves and other barrier precautions. Similar recommendations are made for morticians, dialysis technicians, laboratory and housekeeping personnel.

Where important safety precautions are not exercised by employers, some health care providers have been forced to take the issue into their own hands. In a controversial worker's compensation case in San Francisco, Norma Watson, a nurse at San Francisco General Hospital, sued her employers after she developed an ulcer because she was told to handle AIDS patients without a protective mask or gloves. The nurse won a $5000 disability payment. Hospital administrators had ruled that protective clothing was unnecessary.

"I had always had the fear, knowing there is no medicine for the disease," the nurse told reporters at the Los Angeles *Times*.

"They claim [the protective clothing] hurts the sensitive feelings of the patient, but what about the nurse?"

Despite the feelings of patients who must deal with health care workers who are often dressed in protective clothing, it is imperative that the CDC guidelines be followed, both to protect employees and to limit the liability of employers. To preclude liability, consistent monitoring of physicians and other health workers by their employers and their adherence to federal guidelines are necessary and fundamental.

HEALTH CARE WORKERS AND STRESS

The Los Angeles *Times* reports that in San Francisco and throughout the nation, health care workers who have devoted themselves to the care of AIDS patients are experiencing severe stress and "worker burnout." The personal toll to medical personnel caring for AIDS patients has reflected itself differently for different individuals. Marta Ashley, a coordinator for a volunteer group for AIDS patients, said that she gained 35 pounds, spent weeks in therapy, and took time off from work. Steve Abbot, a staff member of a San Francisco hospital, found himself crying uncontrollably during a staff meeting. Linda Maxey, another AIDS care worker, felt herself near exhaustion and gave up her hospital job for a two-month backpacking trip in Nepal.

These individuals illustrate the growing problems of stress and anxiety reaction affecting medical personnel who care for AIDS patients. The Los Angeles *Times* put the problem into perspective when it asked, "Who will take care of the care-givers?" These issues are now facing hospitals, institutions, and many of the medical and service organizations that serve patients suffering from the disease.

Signs of stress are visible in people associated with AIDS victims nationwide. One New York internist, Dr. Stephen Caiazza, has said that more than 200 of his patients have died. "It's very difficult to bury patient after patient and realize as a physician you're entirely helpless. . . . After a while a doctor has an over-

whelming sense of impotence." Paul Boneberg, director of Mobi-
lization Against AIDS, a San Francisco political advocacy group,
reported his feelings were like "battle fatigue."

One study found that 56 percent of physicians reported feeling
more stress as a result of working with patients who have the
disease. Fully 46 percent reported an increased personal fear of
death, and 14 percent had begun psychotherapy. The precise impact on health care workers in the field is hard to determine.
Many hospitals with AIDS patients have begun weekly counseling services and group therapy sessions for their employees in
response to this growing trend of "worker burnout."

The problems of exhaustion, depression, anxiety, and feelings
of helplessness are expressed by workers who are *committed* to
the patients they serve. Despite their personal frustrations as
medical professionals in the field, they continue to fight the personal toll associated with caring for others who have the disease.

Fighting Discrimination in Health Care

What, if anything, can a person with AIDS do to fight discrimination by health care workers? If initial efforts at remedying discrimination problems are unsuccessful, litigation may become
necessary. If an institution does not adhere to its community service obligation with respect to patients with AIDS, an adminis-
trative complaint should be filed with the Department of Health
and Human Services Office of Civil Rights. If no action is forth-
coming, legal representation should be obtained.

Where a health provider's treatment of a client falls below ac-
ceptable standards of medical practice, legal action in tort can be
instigated. Tort theories for recovery might include malpractice
(negligence), abandonment, and intentional infliction of emotional distress.

The attorney representing a discriminated-against AIDS pa-
tient may be able to sue on the basis of statutory violations. In
California, the cities of Los Angeles, West Hollywood, and San
Francisco have ordinances that specifically prohibit discrimina-

tion against persons with AIDS. Thus legal action can be brought against persons who refuse to provide medical treatment because of the disease. The Los Angeles ordinance (Los Angeles Municipal Code, 3:5.8), for example, recognizes a private right of action against health care facilities that discriminate against AIDS patients. As a result, a hospital or health care institution that discriminates against someone with the disease faces civil as well as state prosecution.

In addition, laws prohibiting discrimination against the disabled or physically handicapped can be relied on. Although the issue has not yet been specifically tested, Section 504 of the Rehabilitation Act should provide relief from discrimination by a large number of primary health care facilities that receive federal funding, including Medicare and Medicaid. Section 504 provides that "no otherwise qualified handicapped individual . . . shall, solely by reasons of his handicap, be excluded from the participation in, be denied the benefits of, or be subjected to discrimination under any program or activity receiving federal financial assistance." In these facilities, refusal to treat may constitute violation of federal law, and the AIDS patient can seek vindication of his legal rights.

DOCTORS WITH AIDS

As the AIDS epidemic spreads in the population, professionals in many different fields have become infected with the disease. Lawyers, teachers, athletes, politicians, artists, and even doctors have fallen victim to the virus.

The issue of physicians with AIDS treating patients is troublesome for many people, and as the problem comes into the spotlight, institutions and lawmakers will have to make serious and important decisions involving issues of civil rights and public health.

In one recent example of this problem, a doctor practicing medicine at Chicago's Cook County Hospital was ordered to stop seeing patients and suspended from his medical practice when hospital authorities learned that he had the disease. The suspension outraged other physicians. The debate triggered a series of board meetings between Chicago's medical authorities on the state, city, and county levels. The doctor was eventually restricted to research, office work, and supervisory capacities pending a final disposition of the case. In the interim the physician was prohibited from seeing patients or performing surgery.

The doctor's lawyer, Harvey Grossman of the American Civil Liberties Union, is preparing a lawsuit in federal court against the hospital that charges violation of the Vocational Rehabilitation Act and the Fourteenth Amendment. The suit seeks $1 million in compensatory and punitive damages. Despite the threatened legal actions, one spokesman for the Cooke County medical board stated that one discrimination lawsuit that would cost the hospital $100,000 was a small price to pay compared to the cost of risking exposure of the disease to the hospital's patients.

Doctors in support of the terminated physician argue that if CDC guidelines are closely followed, the infected doctor poses no risk whatsoever to his patients or fellow workers. Medical authorities in Chicago disagree, claiming that even if the real risk is minimal, the risk perceived by the public is very real. Hospital administrators fear loss of business due to panic over the doctor's presence in the hospital. The battle for the physician's reinstatement is still continuing, and the court case may prove to be a landmark decision on employment discrimination. The American Medical Association has taken no official stance on the case, and it is considered to be the first case to come to trial testing the adequacy of CDC control guidelines, their legal impact, and the duties of a hospital as employer and public health provider.

Liability in Blood Transfusion

The following groups of persons are currently known to be at high risk for developing AIDS, according to the Centers for Disease Control:

- Sexually active homosexual and bisexual men—71 percent of AIDS cases

- Intravenous drug abusers who share needles—21 percent of AIDS cases
- Heterosexuals who have intercourse with people who are seropositive or at high risk—2 percent of AIDS cases
- Hemophiliacs who have received contaminated blood-clotting factor products—1 percent of AIDS cases
- Other people who have received transfusions of contaminated blood—2 percent of AIDS cases
- Newborn infants of infected mothers or newborn infants who have received transfusions—1 percent of AIDS cases

Although the number of persons who have contracted the disease through transfusions of blood is relatively small compared to the other AIDS risk groups (over 20,000 cases have been reported in homosexual males and intravenous drug users, compared to fewer than 500 transfusion cases reported to the CDC), the group infected in this manner has grown steadily. Infants account for 10 percent of these cases.

Despite new efforts at screening, small quantities of tainted blood continue to slip through. The chances of being infected with AIDS from blood that has been screened is now 64,000 to 1. Studies have reported several cases in which the virus failed to show up when the blood was originally screened but became apparent six months later after transfusion to a hospital patient.

An estimated 3 million blood transfusions are given to hospital patients each year, and the number of those patients who will develop AIDS is very small.

Who falls into this new risk category? The group of AIDS patients who have been infected with the virus through transfusions are individuals who have been recipients of blood generally connected with surgery. The median age of the group is 54. Men and women are represented equally, and most victims are Caucasians.

The American Red Cross suggests that to reduce the risk of contamination, patients should permit blood transfusion only when absolutely necessary or donate their own blood before surgery.

The Red Cross accounts for half of the 12 million units of blood collected each year. It makes every effort to minimize the danger of using contaminated blood by screening donors. In addition, doctors attempt to lower the risk by discouraging people in high-risk groups from giving blood. However, some people can initially test negative for exposure to the virus and later develop the disease. The problem is increased by the time lag between infection with the virus and development of antibodies in the blood, a period of several weeks to several months.

Although hospitals and blood manufacturers who administer tainted blood can be sued, legal recovery is difficult. The situations are analogous to the cases involving infection with hepatitis B through blood transfusions, and many plaintiffs in these cases have found the courts unwilling to impose legal liability on blood suppliers.

On June 4, 1987, the California senate acted to ease this problem by voting in favor of a bill that makes it a crime for an AIDS carrier to donate blood when he knows he has the disease. Under the bill, it would be a felony punishable by six years in state prison. A number of other states are also considering such measures.

LEGAL RECOVERY

A legal claim against a hospital or blood bank that provides infected blood would be based on the laws of product liability. These rules permit consumers of products to recover in tort for injuries or harm caused by an unfit product placed in the stream of commerce. The plaintiff infected with AIDS would base his lawsuit on the contention that the hospital or blood bank supplied an unfit product for patient use.

A victim of transfusion-related AIDS may pursue recovery for injuries under three legal theories. One is a concept lawyers call "strict liability," which places legal liability on the *manufacturer or supplier* of the defective blood. A claim for "breach of implied warranty" involves liability on a *seller* in cases where unfit goods are sold. Finally, a claim of negligence can be brought against the defendant for inadequate blood *testing* or blood donor *screening*.

State laws differ, as explained more fully below, and recovery based on the theories of breach of implied warranty and strict liability will be successful in only a few states. Further, actions in negligence will present problems of proof, including the identification of the source of transmission. In one recent case, *South Florida Blood Service Inc. v. Rasmussen,* the court refused to order the disclosure of blood donors. The state's interest in maintaining a public blood supply and confidentiality of donors outweighed the individual's need to seek the identity of such donors.

Further, the timing of the injury is important. In determining the legal liability of blood banks or hospitals that supplied infected blood, it is necessary to distinguish cases in which tainted blood was received before the development of screening tests for the HIV antibody from situations involving cases arising after the availability of the tests.

BLOOD DONOR SCREENING

The ELISA HIV antibody test, developed in 1985, permits groups like the American Red Cross and other organizations that collect blood to screen donations for the AIDS antibody. Rules developed by the CDC and implemented by the Food and Drug Administration make such testing mandatory. Blood that is found to test positive in the initial screening cannot be used in transfusions.

Experts believe that the ELISA test is more than 99 percent accurate. There is some risk, however, that blood that tests negative for the disease may still carry HIV. Studies have reported several cases in which the antibody was not detected in ELISA-based screening but appeared six months later. Blood from an asymptomatic carrier may not produce a positive ELISA test result. Therefore, a blood supplier or doctor administering blood must inform prospective patients of the *continuing risk* of these products.

BREACH OF IMPLIED WARRANTY

Under the legal theory of breach of implied warranty, the Uniform Commercial Code (laws governing commercial transactions adopted in all 50 states) imposes liability on the seller of any product "not of merchantable quality." In the case of the sale of blood, the seller is bound by an implied warranty that the blood is free of harmful infectious agents and is fit for human transfusion.

Legal recovery requires the sale of a product. Are blood transfusions a sale under the Uniform Commercial Code? No. Most courts have ruled that blood transfusions constitute a service, not a sale of a product.

In only two states, Florida and New Jersey, have courts been willing to consider blood transfusion a sale of a product. These lawsuits involved blood infected with hepatitis B, and plaintiffs were permitted to recover under the theory of implied warranty when blood was found to be contaminated. No AIDS-linked blood transfusion case involving the implied warranty theory has yet been resolved by the courts, but significant similarities exist between hepatitis B and AIDS.

In response to the increasing litigation regarding transfusion-related infection with hepatitis, most states enacted "blood immunity" statutes that shield blood suppliers from legal liability. These rules provide that as a matter of state law the supplying of blood is to be considered a service and not a sale of a commodity. These laws make blood suppliers and hospitals immune from legal accountability for the transmission of infection via transfused blood. In these states the recipient of a tainted blood transfusion is unable to pursue recovery.

The only jurisdictions in which a plaintiff who received contaminated blood can pursue relief are Florida, New Jersey, Rhode Island, Vermont, and the District of Columbia. In all other states, laws grant immunity to hospitals and blood banks from legal liability involving tainted blood.

STRICT LIABILITY

The primary goal of strict liability is to compensate innocent victims for injuries or damages from the manufacturer who put dangerous products on the market. The rule recognizes that the manufacturer is in the best position to insure against the threat of injury from a defective product by making it safe in the first place. The rules motivate manufacturers to design and make safe products that in theory will reduce the cost to society of product-related injuries.

An alternative basis in legal recovery for an action against a hospital or blood bank might be strict liability in tort. The American Law Institute's *Restatement (Second) of Torts* provides that strict liability should apply to sellers "who sell any product in a defective condition unreasonably dangerous to the user or consumer . . . [even if] the seller has exercised all possible care in the preparation and sale of his product."

In 1985 a hemophiliac who contracted AIDS from a blood clotting agent was denied the right to legal recovery based on strict liability. The California Sixth District Court of Appeal held that the blood immunity statute precluded recovery. In *Hyland Therapeutic* v. *Superior Court* the defendant was not a hospital or a blood bank. It manufactured a blood clotting factor developed to correct bleeding episodes. The court rejected the plaintiff's distinction that the defendant in the case was a blood manufacturer and not a hospital or blood bank. The court found that the clotting agent manufacturer should be afforded the same protections as hospitals under the blood immunity statutes. The blood recipient was found to have received a service, not a product for sale. The plaintiff was unable to recover under a strict liability theory for the infection with the AIDS virus, and as a result he was denied any legal relief.

It has been suggested that the blood immunity statutes be amended to allow imposition of strict liability for infection with AIDS through tainted blood. Transfusion recipients cannot detect impurities in the blood before they receive it and cannot guard against injury short of refusing to receive the transfusion. It is the hospital or blood bank that has the means to detect impure blood, so it seems reasonable to hold hospitals and blood suppliers strictly liable for transfusion-related infections.

In some states blood immunity statutes have been held not to apply in situations involving blood banks. These courts reasoned that providing blood by a blood bank is considered a sale and that the doctrines of strict liability and implied warranty thus do apply. These courts have distinguished blood banks as manufacturers of a product for sale as opposed to hospitals, which provide medical services. In these states an AIDS victim can pursue legal recovery against a blood bank under a strict liability theory.

The blood processing statutes were enacted to promote the public health by ensuring sufficient blood supplies. In states where these rules have been made into law, courts continue to support the statutes.

Affordable health care is a national concern, and blood immunity statutes are seen by many lawmakers as a necessary evil in shielding hospitals and blood banks from enormous liability payments in transfusion-related injuries. Courts are likely to continue the trend of supporting the blood immunity statutes. It will preclude recovery in strict liability and implied warranty for blood recipients in most states who contract AIDS, as it has already in analogous cases involving hepatitis B.

NEGLIGENCE

Plaintiffs who have been denied legal recovery on an implied warranty or strict liability basis may choose to pursue an action in negligence. Under certain circumstances a hospital might be held liable for negligence in administering impure blood. Such liability has been found in cases involving hepatitis B. The similarities between hepatitis B and AIDS in the context of tainted blood suggest that courts faced with AIDS transmission cases will follow the precedent established in hepatitis B cases.

To recover under a theory of negligence (review the basic elements in Chapter Two) a plaintiff must prove that a standard of care existed, that the defendant's conduct fell below that standard, and that the defendant's conduct was the proximate cause of the plaintiff's injury.

In an AIDS-tainted-blood case, the plaintiff would have to show that the hospital or blood supplier failed to act reasonably in carrying out the standard of care it owed the patient. One of the critical elements in establishing this fact would be the issue of blood testing.

To establish liability the plaintiff must show that proper screening measures were either *not* employed or were employed *negligently*. This means that if the transfusion took place after 1985, when the ELISA test became available, the plaintiff would have to show that the defendant hospital failed to follow CDC recommendations to provide high-risk donor screening and voluntary abstention by members of high-risk groups.

Naturally, to recover in negligence causation must be established: The blood recipient must prove that the disease was contracted through the transfusion. This burden might be met by eliminating the possibility of other causes of AIDS; for example, the patient might submit evidence that he is not an intravenous drug user, a homosexual or bisexual, or a member of any other high-risk group. The nature of the disease and its symptoms will also assist in proving causation, and medical experts should be called to testify about their opinions regarding the source of transmission.

The nation's first trial testing a blood bank's liability for transmission of AIDS ended in settlement. The amount could not be disclosed, the plaintiff's attorney stated, but it "was something less than the $2 million sought" by his client, a 72-year-old San Francisco woman.

The blood transfusions took place in 1983, more than a year and a half before routine blood screening began. At the time, the blood bank was relying on questionnaires to screen donors. Attorneys for the blood bank admitted that some of the blood used in the transfusion had come from a male homosexual who had not completed the questionnaire.

Because the case ended before a jury verdict was reached, the trial did not settle the issue of blood bank liability. But it could set an important trend. At least 20 similar cases are now pending.

Once a plaintiff has met his burden as to causation and demonstrated that the defendant failed to exercise a reasonable standard of care by administering contaminated blood, the plaintiff may seek an appropriate damage award as compensation for his injuries.

INFORMED CONSENT AND MISREPRESENTATION

In some cases a duty to act reasonably may encompass obtaining informed consent from a patient before administering the transfusion of blood. This may be especially true for AIDS antibody testing because of the possibility of a false-negative result due to the time lag in the incubation period of the virus. Also, if blood has been obtained from paid blood donors, a patient should be informed of the increased risk attached to that blood. Three states—California, Georgia, and Illinois—have enacted statutes that require that blood obtained from paid donors be so labeled.

Even if a patient has given written consent to a blood transfusion, this consent will not necessarily prevent the patient from instigating legal action later. The consent is effective only if the blood supplier or hospital has done all that is reasonably necessary to ensure that the blood is free from infection. Only after the blood has been tested for the AIDS antibody and donors have been screened for membership in high-risk groups can a plaintiff's informed consent absolve liability.

In summary, three possible forms of recovery exist for a patient who is a victim of an AIDS-infected blood transfusion: negligence, strict liability, and breach of implied warranty. State laws generally preclude hospital or blood bank liability in each of these forms except negligence. Unless states reform blood immunity laws and change the characterization of blood transfusion from a service to a sale, strict liability and implied warranty actions will not provide legal relief. However, if the AIDS victim can demonstrate that standards for blood testing or donor screening existed but were not used, the patient may be able to pursue legal relief in negligence.

Mandatory Disclosure: Honesty Between Lovers

The suit by Marc Christian, Rock Hudson's lover, against the actor's estate illustrates some of the points raised in this book.

Christian had been living with Hudson for several years when he began noticing definite changes in the actor's appearance, including a substantial loss of weight. When Marc asked his lover whether he was ill—and finally whether he had AIDS—Hudson emphatically denied it. Not until nine months after that denial did Christian learn from a radio broadcast that Hudson did in fact have the disease.

In an article in the *New York Times Magazine* on May 3, 1987, Sara Davidson, Hudson's biographer, said that for Hudson, all-important career considerations led him to make "some questionable decisions." One of them was to keep his illness a secret from his lover "because Rock feared Christian would tell others." Hudson was afraid that if it became known that he was homosexual, this would ruin his career. That, to him, was more important than anything else.

Christian, in his lawsuit, claimed that he had been suffering extreme and constant fear that he was in danger of receiving a "death sentence."

In an appearance on a *Donahue* show in 1985, Marvin Mitchelson, Christian's attorney, likened the situation to being faced with Russian roulette day after day. Christian, who at this point has shown no evidence of having been infected, might, according to his doctor, still develop the disease any time within the next five years.

On the *Donahue* show, Christian claimed that in his view Hudson was manipulated by several close associates to keep the information from him. In addition to the personal hurt Christian felt, he also thought "there was no consideration that if at any time my relationship with Rock had ended before I knew he had AIDS, I might have ended up with someone else, and I might have exposed [him]. It could have been a chain reaction. Nobody took any kind of consideration that people might have been exposed unknowingly."

Christian's lawsuit involves a $20 million claim against Rock Hudson's estate. The suit asks for $10 million in general damages for negligence, bodily injury, mental distress, fraud, and deceit. A separate $10 million claim against Hudson's estate is for infliction of emotional distress, bodily injury, fraud, and deceit. Christian is also seeking $1 million from four of Hudson's intimates and advisers who, he claims, conspired with the actor to keep his condition a secret.

If Christian can prove that Hudson knowingly and deliberately misled him and placed him in danger of contracting the disease, Christian stands a good chance of winning a case in fraud, deceit, and mental distress. If Christian can prove that Hudson caused him physical harm, he may also recover in negligence. The case will be watched with great interest by the legal profession as well as by other victims of STDs.

Final Thoughts

AIDS is still in its infancy, and the experts don't talk about it with the assurances that inspire total confidence. The disease has an aura of mystery, of evil, and it instills terror even in people considered at low risk. We all feel threatened, which is no doubt the reason AIDS has been getting the lion's share of media attention.

Because it can cause death and because, in the United States, it primarily affects homosexuals and drug addicts, AIDS has stirred the most controversy. Opinions range all the way from people who consider it God's rightful punishment for perversion and would ship all people at risk to a desert island, to those who feel that the victims' suffering is so severe that no effort should be spared to help them, whatever the consequences to the public at large.

The heat generated by the topic was illustrated on a *Nightline* program on July 2, 1987, dealing with the criminal prosecution of people with AIDS. Los Angeles lawyer Gloria Allred defended the AIDS victims, claiming that the stress induced by their illness, combined with society's attitude, was driving them to desperate acts. Los Angeles District Attorney Ira Reiner (who is prosecuting Joseph Edward Markowski for attempted murder because the man, knowing he had AIDS, sold his blood), argued that the safety of the general public is paramount; anyone who endangers it must be held accountable to the full extent of the law. Harvard University law professor Arthur Miller took what might be interpreted as a middle course: He felt that the law needed to be recast to allow for fair treatment of people with AIDS and to develop alternate ways of dealing with them. Using the "heavy hammer of the law" against these people would only drive them underground, to the detriment of everyone, he concluded.

Has anyone the right, no matter how great the psychological pressure, knowingly to endanger others? That is, I think, the ethical question we all have to face—with AIDS, but also with every other communicable disease, including all STDs. And are we willing to leave a decision that may affect us for the rest of our lives in the hands of someone driven to despair and perhaps irrationality?

Serious as the AIDS crisis is, most sexually active people stand in far, far greater risk of contracting any of the other STDs. In addition, the legal problems AIDS presents are no different from those of genital herpes or any of the other STDs—except, of course, that the transmitters of syphilis or chlamydia are unlikely to face criminal prosecution, certainly not for murder.

Does the fact that other STDs are not usually fatal lessen your moral obligation toward your lover, and his or her next lover, and that lover's next lover? Can you still afford to go on in the same old way?

I don't think that any decent, humane person would take the position that others don't matter. But for those who would seriously advocate such indifference, the risk, not only to others but to themselves as well, would only increase.

I have neither the desire nor the intention to encourage litigation between lovers. What I set out to do in this book was to show everyone what might be in store for sexually active people who mislead their partners—out of shyness, laziness, cowardice, malice, or for whatever reason. This is a tool, if it be needed, to discourage all those little white lies so many of us are apt to utter or to imply by our failure to speak out. I also want it to be a warning to those who, with malice aforethought, set out to hurt others.

What I want, in short, is to bring lovers to the point where they can really believe those promises in the dark.

APPENDIXES

Appendix I: STDs: Estimated New Cases for 1988

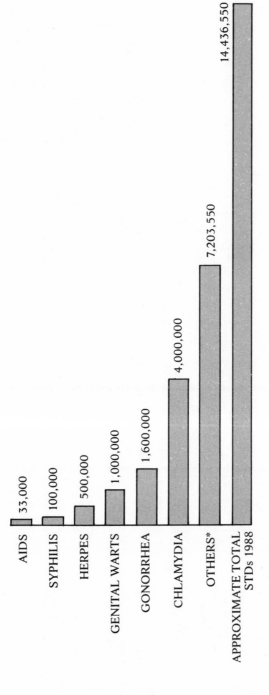

Source: Centers For Disease Control

*Others=Hepatitis B, Vaginosis (Gardnerella), Chancroid, Lymphogranuloma Inguinale, Nongonococcal Urethritis, Molluscum Contagiosum, Granuloma Inguinale, Mucopurulent Cervicitis, and others.

Appendix II: Medical Review Charts

AIDS

Definition and Outcome	Symptoms	Detection	Prevention and Treatment	General Information*
Blood lymphocyte infection with human immunodeficiency virus (HIV).	Fatigue, weakness, swollen glands, sore throat, skin rash, night sweats and headache.	Blood tests (serology):	*Prevention:*	Infected are 71% bisexual and homosexual males; 13% intravenous drug abusers (IVDA) who share needles and syringes; 8% homosexual IVDAs. Balance are hemophiliacs and others who received infected transfusions or blood products, or children infected at birth; this includes females.
Causes profound abnormalities of T helper cells.	Diarrhea and weight loss then follow.	1. ELISA—sensitive and specific but still false-positives (Ab) (more than 99% accurate).	1. High-risk group must limit number of sex partners or abstain if HIV Ab status is unknown.	
Attacks the body's immune system and impairs ability to fight disease.	Shortness of breath. Easy tiring. Frequent infections. Chronic cough, unexplained fever.	2. Western blot test *must be done* if ELISA result is positive (Ab).	2. If HIV negative, safe sex is *only* possible with HIV-negative partner.	United States has more than 47,022
Creates susceptibility to:	Unusual and multiple skin growths and bruising.	All people in high-risk groups should be tested.	3. If HIV positive, must seek medical care and abstain	
1. Multiple opportunistic infections.				

2. Kaposi's sarcoma (rare skin cancer) and other malignancies.

3. *Pneumocystis carinii* pneumonia (PCP).

Exposure to STDs and other bacterial, viral, or protozoal infections may trigger multiplication of the dormant virus.

Retest periodically because seroconversion can occur 3 to 6 months after exposure.

Should be done in patients with unusual chronic medical problems.

Positive results are *not* diagnostic of AIDS but indicate virus infection or prior exposure.

from sex because of high risk.

4. Avoid sharing body fluids and semen.

5. Avoid exposure to blood products.

6. Avoid shared needles.

7. Education and counseling activities

Treatment:

Retrovir (Burroughs Wellcome) now widely available by prescription. Preliminary: Antigen levels drop as patient's condition improves.

Ribavarin by Viratek/ICN. Delays progression to AIDS in

cases and 26,714 deaths since November 23, 1987, with 57% mortality since June 1981. Estimated to be 100% fatal.

An estimated 1.0 to 1.5 million people are infected in the United States today.

Federal guidelines for testing and reporting have been issued and are being circulated for comment.

Patients should be counseled by physician about risks of inadvertent disclosure of test results.

Health care workers must exercise cau-

AIDS (continued)

Definition and Outcome	Symptoms	Detection	Prevention and Treatment	General Information*
			lymphadenopathy syndrome (LAS).	tion and follow CDC and federal guidelines.
			This is a deadly, incurable contagious disease. *There is at present no known cure.*	*Pandemic.*

* Statistics derived from reports issued by The Centers for Disease Control, the Institute of Medicine National Academy of Sciences, the Pan American Health Organization, and the World Health Organization. Total number of cases for nonreportable diseases is very difficult to derive. Therefore some of the figures here are estimates from early and incomplete reporting to the CDC and national surveys conducted by CDC and Emory University.

Hepatitis B

Definition and Outcome	Symptoms	Detection	Prevention and Treatment	General Information*
Infection with hepatitis B virus.	Nausea and vomiting, loss of appetite, profound and prolonged fatigue.	Blood chemistries for enzymes ALT and AST.	*Prevention:* Avoid sexual promiscuity.	There are 200 million carriers worldwide.
May be the major cause of liver cancer.	Yellow skin, diarrhea, dark urine and light stools.	ELISA AUSAB for viral antibodies.	*Treatment:*	Twenty percent of population in Asia infected, 0.1% of population in the United States, with 200,000 new cases per year.
		ELISA AUSZYME for viral surface antigens (Abbott Diagnostics).	Inoculation with Hepatitis-B (MSD) immune globulin immediately after exposure or up to 2 weeks before.	
		ELISA CORE for viral antibodies.		Homosexuals and IVDAs at high risk. Heterosexuals at lower risk.
		ELISA COREZYME M for IGM (specific recent infection).	Prior vaccination with Heptavax-B (MSD) in high-risk individuals.	This is a major worldwide public health problem.
			Antibiotics are ineffective.	Mandatory reporting in all states.
			There is no cure.	*Epidemic.*

* Statistics derived from reports issued by The Centers for Disease Control, the Institute of Medicine National Academy of Sciences, the Pan American Health Organization, and the World Health Organization. Total number of cases for nonreportable diseases is very difficult to derive. Therefore some of the figures here are estimates from early and incomplete reporting to the CDC and national surveys conducted by CDC and Emory University.

203

Chlamydia

Definition and Outcome	Symptoms	Detection	Prevention and Treatment	General Information*
Infection with *Chlamydia trachomatis* micro-organism.	Genital discharge, spotting, vaginal itching and burning, fatigue, flulike symptoms, burning urination, pelvic pain, and low-grade fever.	Fluorescent monoclonal antibody test (Syva Microtrak-Syntex).	*Prevention:* Stay with one partner. Both get tested and retested after treatment is completed.	Occurs in healthy, young, sexually active women, and their partners.
Present with other bacteria in 50% of pelvic inflammatory diseases (PIDs).	Eighty percent may have no symptoms until serious complications occur.	ELISA CHLAMYDIZYME—80% accuracy (Abbott Diagnostics)—urogenital swab.	Regular follow-ups after cure whether or not symptoms develop.	Can also be transmitted to household members, with no sexual contact.
Causes 50% of nongonococcal urethritis in males (NGU).		Cell culture—very accurate but expensive.	Avoid exposure to other people's body fluids.	True incidence is increasing.
Causes mucopurulent cervicitis.		Urinalysis for white blood cells (pus cells).	Use condoms and other sexual barrier protection.	Most prevalent STD in United States.
High risk of ectopic (tubal) pregnancy and sterility.		Testing should be done once each year for healthy, young, sexually active	Exercise careful hygiene always.	Estimated 4 million new cases per year, although true extent and total number of cases is not known.
Can cause infection in newborn and blindness if not treated.				Now reportable in 40 states.

204

Causes 50% of estimated 500,000 cases of acute epididymitis (testes) treated in the United States each year.

Treatment:

Best antibiotics: ampicillin and tetracycline in combination therapy.

women, their partners, and other household members with no sexual contact.

Both partners should be tested for other STDs.

Active PID cases require 4 to 5 days of intravenous antibiotics.

There is a cure.

Epidemic.

* Statistics derived from reports issued by The Centers for Disease Control, the Institute of Medicine National Academy of Sciences, the Pan American Health Organization, and the World Health Organization. Total number of cases for nonreportable diseases is very difficult to derive. Therefore some of the figures here are estimates from early and incomplete reporting to the CDC and national surveys conducted by CDC and Emory University.

205

Genital Herpes

Definition and Outcome	Symptoms	Detection	Prevention and Treatment	General Information*
Infection with herpes simplex virus.	Painful anal and genital blisters and ulcers of skin and mucous membranes.	For accurate diagnosis gynecologists should do:	*Prevention:*	Estimated total of cases in the United States: 10 million with up to 500,000 new cases per year.
HSV-1—cold sore/fever blister. HSV-2—genital sore/blister.	Fever, muscle aching, fatigue, and headache.	1. Colposcopy.	Avoid sexual contact when lesions are present.	Difficult to avoid.
Both types now occur in both locations.	There are warning symptoms of tingling, headache, and soreness before recurrence.	2. Cancer (Pap) smear.	Use condoms and spermicidal jellies because of asymptomatic viral shedding, although this is not fully protective.	Seventy-five percent of cases transmitted unknowingly by partner unaware of infection.
May cause life-threatening infection: 50% of newborns die; 50% of survivors suffer serious mental deficit.	Subsequent attacks are milder.	3. Fluorescent monoclonal antibody test.	*Treatment:*	Now reportable in 25 states.
Implicated in cancer of the cervix (epidemiology).		4. Cell culture.	Zovirax (acyclovir) from Burroughs Wellcome stops viral replication at infection site and delays recurrence.	*Epidemic.*
Women bear an especially heavy burden		5. Test for other STDs.	The CO_2 laser kills the virus at infection	

206

because of reproductive complications.

Most people develop latent or chronic infection after first attack.

Stress causes recurrence.

site and lessens frequency and severity of recurrence.

Antibiotics do not work.

Counseling is very important.

There is no cure.

---

* Statistics derived from reports issued by The Centers for Disease Control, the Institute of Medicine National Academy of Sciences, the Pan American Health Organization, and the World Health Organization. Total number of cases for nonreportable diseases is very difficult to derive. Therefore some of the figures here are estimates from early and incomplete reporting to the CDC and national surveys conducted by CDC and Emory University.

Genital Warts

Definition and Outcome	Symptoms	Detection	Prevention and Treatment	General Information*
Infection with human papilloma virus (HPV).	Itching, small superficial genital growths.	For very accurate diagnosis, gynecologist must do:	*Prevention:* Stay with one partner who has been diagnosed as free of infection.	Number 1 viral STD in United States.
Affects internal and external genitals.	Causes painful intercourse and soreness.	1. Colposcopy examination.	Both partners must be treated and diagnosed as free of infection.	True extent and total number of cases unknown, but estimate is 1 million cases per year in United States.
Affects epidermis (skin) and mucous membranes.	Symptoms may be absent.	2. Cancer (Pap) smear.	Periodic reexamination is necessary because of high persistence and to avoid recurrence.	There are more than 50 virus types.
Strongly implicated in cervical and other genital tract cancers in both sexes.	Occurs in and around the rectum.	3. Directed biopsies.		Not reportable.
	Causes body warts.	4. DNA probe direct smear.	*Treatment:* CO_2 laser is treatment of choice. Less than 2% recurrence rate.	*Epidemic.*
Implicated in higher number of deaths from invasive cancer of the cervix for females under age 35.		There is no blood test for HPV.		
Can be fatal in newborn by obstruction of the upper airway.		Both partners can and should be examined, and periodically reexamined by gynecologist, to prevent reinfection.		

Highly infectious.

Test for other STDs. They occur together and can be treated with combined antibiotic therapy.

Not reportable.

Traditional superficial treatments are generally ineffective, painful, with high failure rate. They can also be toxic (podophyllin).

Close follow-up with gynecologist who is an expert in colposcopy advisable because this is a recurrent premalignant disease.

There is a cure.

* Statistics derived from reports issued by The Centers for Disease Control, the Institute of Medicine National Academy of Sciences, the Pan American Health Organization, and the World Health Organization. Total number of cases for nonreportable diseases is very difficult to derive. Therefore some of the figures here are estimates from early and incomplete reporting to the CDC and national surveys conducted by CDC and Emory University.

Gonorrhea

Definition and Outcome	Symptoms	Detection	Prevention and Treatment	General Information*
Infection with *Neisseria gonorrhoeae* bacterium.	Yellow genital discharge (pus), plus painful urination in males and pelvic pain in females.	Endocervical culture and sensitivity test in women.	*Prevention:* Look for genital discharge before sex.	Estimated total of cases in United States: 1.8 million, with 900,000 new cases estimated in 1987.
Incubation: 2 to 8 days.	Females often asymptomatic.	ELISA GONO-ZYME (Abbott). Urogenital swab.	Use condoms and spermicidal jelly, though not 100% safe.	Mandatory reporting in all states.
High risk of pelvic inflammatory disease (PID).		Gram stain endocervix.	Regular follow-up and tests after treatment is completed.	*Epidemic.*
Eye infection in newborn can lead to blindness if not treated promptly.		Urethral culture and sensitivity in males.	Stay with one partner.	
Advanced cases develop arthritis.		Pharyngeal and rectal cultures and sensitivity in men and women.	*Treatment:* Best antibiotics: ampicillin and tetracycline in combination.	
High risk of ectopic pregnancy and sterility.			*There is a cure.*	

* Statistics derived from reports issued by The Centers for Disease Control, the Institute of Medicine National Academy of Sciences, the Pan American Health Organization, and the World Health Organization. Total number of cases for nonreportable diseases is very difficult to derive. Therefore some of the figures here are estimates from early and incomplete reporting to the CDC and national surveys conducted by CDC and Emory University.

Syphilis

Definition and Outcome	Symptoms	Detection	Prevention and Treatment	General Information*
Infection with spirochete of *Treponema pallidum*.	Painless oral and genital ulcers (chancre).	Blood tests:	*Prevention:*	Total number of cases in United States estimated to be 90,000 in 1987; up 33% between 1986 and 1987.
Very contagious, destructive, and deadly disease.	Sore throat and/or rash.	1. VDRL (STS).	Use of:	
	Lesions often occur in and around the rectum.	2. TPHA (RBC test).	1. Condoms and caps.	
Has silent, insidious course.	Symptoms are legion.	3. FTA-ABS (specific).	2. Diaphragm and sponges.	Sixty-six percent of cases are homosexual males.
Damage is irreversible.	Called "the great masquerader."	4. TP-ELISA AF-ELISA (both very specific).	3. Chemical spermicides.	Female share increased almost 5% in 1986.
Central nervous system effects are devastating.		5. Direct smear from lesion.	*Treatment:*	
Cardiovascular damage is profound.			Best antibiotics: penicillin G and tetracycline.	Congenital syphilis (infection with severe damage to newborn) increased 9.5% in 1986.
			Regular follow-up blood test every 3 months for 2 years is imperative.	

211

Syphilis (continued)

Definition and Outcome	Symptoms	Detection	Prevention and Treatment	General Information*
			Cannot repair damage to major organ systems.	Mandatory reporting in all states.
			There is a cure.	*Epidemic.*

* Statistics derived from reports issued by The Centers for Disease Control, the Institute of Medicine National Academy of Sciences, the Pan American Health Organization, and the World Health Organization. Total number of cases for nonreportable diseases is very difficult to derive. Therefore some of the figures here are estimates from early and incomplete reporting to the CDC and national surveys conducted by CDC and Emory University.

Appendix III: State-by-State Legal Guide of Relevant Statutes

ALABAMA

Communicable Disease Statute

Ala. Code § 22-16-17. Transmission of Disease to Another Person.

Any person afflicted with a venereal disease who shall transmit, or assume the risk of transmitting, or do any act which will probably or likely transmit such venereal disease to another person shall be guilty of a misdemeanor and, on conviction, shall be fined not less than $10.00 nor more than $100.00 and may, at the discretion of the court trying the case, be sentenced to hard labor for the county for a term not to exceed six months. (Acts 1919, No. 658, p. 909; Code 1923, § 4380; Code 1940, T. 22, § 275.)

Sodomy Law

Ala. Code § 13A-6-65 (1975):

(a) A person commits the crime of sexual misconduct if . . . [h]e or she engages in deviate sexual intercourse with another person under circumstances other than those covered by sections 6-63 (forced sodomy) and 13A-6-64 (child molestation). Consent no defense to a prosecution under this subdivision.

(b) Sexual misconduct is a Class A misdemeanor.

Ala. Code § 13A-6-60(2) (1975):

Deviate Sexual Intercourse. Any act of sexual gratification between persons not married to each other, involving the sex organ of one person and the mouth or anus of another.

Ala. Code § 13-5-7 (1975):

(a) Sentences for misdemeanors shall be a definite term of imprisonment in the county jail or to hard labor for the county within the following limitations: . . . (1) For a Class A misdemeanor not more than one year.

ARIZONA

Communicable Disease Statutes

Ariz. Rev. Stat. Ann. § 36-631. Person with Contagious or Infectious Disease Exposing Himself to Public; Classification; Exception

A person who knowingly exposes himself or another afflicted with a contagious or infectious disease in a public place or thoroughfare, except in the necessary removal of such person in a manner least dangerous to the public health, is guilty of a class 2 misdemeanor.

Ariz. Rev. Stat. Ann. § 13-707. Sentence of Imprisonment for Misdemeanor

A sentence of imprisonment for a misdemeanor shall be for a definite term to be served other than a place within custody of the department of corrections. The court shall fix the term of imprisonment within the following maximum limitations:

1. For a class 1 misdemeanor, six months.
2. For a class 2 misdemeanor, four months.
3. For a class 3 misdemeanor, thirty days.

§ 13-802 B.

A sentence to pay a fine for a class 2 misdemeanor shall be a sentence to pay an amount, fixed by the court, not more than seven hundred fifty dollars.

Sodomy Law

Ariz. Rev. Stat. Ann. § 13-1411. Crime Against Nature;
Classification

A person who knowingly and without force commits the infamous crime against nature with an adult is guilty of a class 3 misdemeanor.
Amended by Laws 1983, Ch. 202, § 11; Laws 1985, Ch. 364, § 22, eff. May 16, 1985.

Ariz. Rev. Stat. Ann. § 13-707 (1978):

A sentence of imprisonment for a misdemeanor shall be for a definite term to be served other than a place within custody of the department of corrections. The court shall fix the term of imprisonment within the following maximum limitations: . . . For a class 3 misdemeanor, thirty days.

ARKANSAS

Sodomy Law

Ark. Stat. Ann. § 41-1813 (1975):

(1) A person commits sodomy if such person performs any act of sexual gratification involving: (a) the penetration, however slight, of the anus or mouth of an animal or a person by the penis of a person of the same sex or an animal; or (b) the penetration, however slight, of the vagina or anus of an animal or a person by any body member of a person of the same sex or an animal.
(2) Sodomy is a class "A" misdemeanor.

Ark. Stat. Ann. § 41-901 (2)(a) (1981):

A defendant convicted of a misdemeanor may be sentenced according to the following limitations: . . . For a class A misdemeanor, the sentence shall not exceed one (1) year.

CALIFORNIA

Communicable Disease Statute

Calif. Stat. § 3198 (West). Acts in Violation
of Article as Misdemeanor

Any person who refuses to give any information to make any report, to comply with any proper control measure or examination, or to perform any other duty or act required by this article, or who violates any provision of this article or any rule or regulation of the state board issued pursuant to this article, or who exposes any person to or infects any person with any venereal disease; or any person infected with a venereal disease in an infectious state who knows of such condition and who marries or has sexual intercourse, is guilty of a misdemeanor.

Calif. Penal Code § 19. [Punishment for Misdemeanor]

Except in cases where a different punishment is prescribed by any law of this state, every offense declared to be a misdemeanor is punishable by imprisonment in the county jail not exceeding six months, or by fine not exceeding one thousand dollars ($1,000), or by both.

COLORADO

Communicable Disease Statutes

Colo. Rev. Stat. Ann. § 25-4-401. Venereal Diseases.

(1) Syphilis, gonorrhea, chancroid, granuloma inguinale, and lymphogranuloma venereum, referred to in this part 4 as "venereal diseases," are declared to be contagious, infectious, communicable, and dangerous to the public health.

(2) It is unlawful for any person who has knowledge or reasonable grounds to suspect that he is infected with a venereal disease to willfully expose to or infect another with such a disease or to knowingly perform an act which exposes to or infects another person with a venereal disease.

Colo. Rev. Stat. Ann. § 25-4-407. Penalty.

Any person, firm, or corporation violating any of the provisions of this part 4, other than section 25-4-408, or any lawful rule or regulation made by the department of health pursuant to the authority granted in this part 4 or failing or refusing to obey any lawful order issued by any state, county, or municipal health officer pursuant to the authority granted in this part 4 is guilty of a misdemeanor and, upon conviction thereof, shall be punished by a fine of not more than three hundred dollars, or by imprisonment in the county jail for not more than ninety days, or by both such fine and imprisonment.

DELAWARE

Communicable Disease Statutes

Del. Code Ann. § 701. Enumeration of Venereal Diseases; Exposing Others to Infection.

Syphilis, gonorrhea and chancroid, designated in this chapter as venereal diseases, are declared to be contagious, infectious, communicable and dangerous to the public health. No person infected with these diseases or any of them shall expose another person to infection. (Code 1915, § 740A; 30 Del. Laws, c. 53, §§ 1–6; Code 1935, § 778; 16 Del. C. 1953, § 701.)

Del. Code Ann. § 709. Penalties.

Whoever violates this chapter or any lawful rule or regulation made by the Board under § 706 of this title, or fails or refuses to obey any lawful order issued by any state, county or municipal health officer under this chapter shall be fined not more than $1,000 or imprisoned not more than 1 year, or both. (Code 1915, § 740A; 30 Del. Laws, c. 53, §§ 1–6; 33 Del. Laws, c. 57, § 4; 34 Del. Laws, c. 69, § 1; Code 1935, § 778; 16 Del. C. 1953, § 709.)

DISTRICT OF COLUMBIA

Fornication Law

D.C. Code Ann. § 22-1002. Fornication.

If any unmarried man or woman commits fornication in the District, each shall be fined not more than $300 or imprisoned not more than 6 months, or both. (June 29, 1953, 67 Stat. 99, ch. 150, § 214; 1973 Ed., § 22-1002.)

Sodomy Law

D.C. Code Ann. § 22-3502. Sodomy.

(a) Every person who shall be convicted of taking into his or her mouth or anus the sexual organ of any other person or animal, or who shall be convicted of placing his or her sexual organ in the mouth or anus of any other person or animal, or who shall be convicted of having carnal copulation in an opening of the body except sexual parts with another person, shall be fined not more than $1,000 or be imprisoned for a period not exceeding 10 years.

FLORIDA

Communicable Disease Statutes

Fla. Stat. Ann. § 384.01 (West): Diseases Designated as Venereal Diseases.

Syphilis, gonorrhea, and chancroid are designated as venereal diseases and are declared to be contagious, infectious, communicable, and dangerous to the public health. It is unlawful for any one infected with either of these diseases to expose another to infection.

§ 384.02 Sexual Intercourse with Person Afflicted with Venereal Disease Illegal.

It is unlawful for any female afflicted with any venereal disease, knowing of such condition, to have sexual intercourse with any male person, or for any male person afflicted with any venereal disease, knowing of such condition, to have sexual intercourse with any female.

History.—s. 2, ch. 7829, 1919; CGL 3948

§ 384.03 Penalty for Violation.

Any person who shall violate any of the provisions of s. 384.01 or s. 384.02, shall be guilty of a misdemeanor of the second degree, punishable as provided in s. 775.082 or s. 775.083.

§ 775.082(4b)

For a misdemeanor of the second degree, by a definite term of imprisonment not exceeding 60 days.

§ 775.083(2e)

$500, when the conviction is of a misdemeanor of the second degree or a noncriminal violation.

Fornication Law

Fla. Stat. § 798.03 (West): Fornication

If any man commits fornication with a woman, each of them shall be guilty of a misdemeanor of the second degree, punishable as provided in § 775.082 or § 775.083. (See Above)

Sodomy Law

Fla. Stat. Ann. § 800.02 (West): Unnatural and Lascivious Act

Whoever commits any unnatural and lascivious act with another person shall be guilty of a misdemeanor of the second degree, punishable as provided in § 775.082 or § 775.083.

Fla. Stat. Ann. § 775.082(4)(b) (West 1976):

A person who has been convicted of a designated misdemeanor may be sentenced as follows: ... For a misdemeanor of the second degree, by a definite term of imprisonment not exceeding 60 days.

Fla. Stat. Ann. § 775.083(1)(e) (West 1983):

Fines for designated crimes and for noncriminal violations shall not exceed: ... $500, when the conviction is of a misdemeanor of the second degree or a noncriminal violation.

GEORGIA

Fornication Law

Ga. Code Ann. § 26-2010 [16-6-18] Fornication

An unmarried person commits the offense of fornication when he voluntarily has sexual intercourse with another person and, upon conviction thereof, shall be punished as for a misdemeanor.

Ga. Code Ann. § 27-2506 [17-10-3] Misdemeanors, How Punished

(a) Except as otherwise provided by law, every crime declared to be a misdemeanor shall be punished either:

(1) By a fine not to exceed $1,000.00 or by confinement in the county or other jail, county correctional institution, or such other places as counties may provide for maintenance of county inmates, for a total term not to exceed 12 months, or both; or

(2) By confinement under the jurisdiction of the Board of Corrections in a state or county correctional institution or such other institution as the Department of Corrections may direct, for a determinate term of months which shall be more than six months but shall not exceed a total term of 12 months.

Sodomy Law

Ga. Code Ann. § 16-6-2 (1982):

(a) A person commits the offense of sodomy when he performs or submits to any sexual act involving the sex organs of one person and the mouth or anus of another. A person commits the offense of aggravated sodomy when he commits sodomy with force and against the will of the other person.

(b) A person convicted of the offense of sodomy shall be punished by imprisonment for not less than one nor more than 20 years. A person convicted of the offense of aggravated sodomy shall be punished by imprisonment for life or by imprisonment for not less than one nor more than 20 years.

IDAHO

Communicable Disease Statutes

Idaho Code § 39-601. Venereal Diseases Enumerated—Exposure of Other Persons Unlawful.

Syphilis, gonorrhea, acquired immunodeficiency syndrome (AIDS), AIDS related complexes (ARC), other manifestations of HTLV-III (human T-cell lymphotrophic virus-type III) infections and chancroid, hereinafter designated as venereal diseases, are hereby declared to be contagious, infectious, communicable and dangerous to public health; and it shall be unlawful for any one [anyone] infected with these diseases or any of them to knowingly or wilfully expose another person to the infection of such diseases. [1921, ch. 200, §§ 1, 6, p. 406; I.C.A., § 38-501; am. 1945, ch. 52, § 1, p. 67; am. 1986, ch. 70, § 1, p. 195.]

§ 39-704. Penalty for Violations.

Any person violating any of the provisions of this chapter shall be punished by a fine of not more than $500.00, or by imprisonment in the county jail for not more than six (6) months or by both such fine and imprisonment. [1921, ch. 201, § 4, p. 408; I.C.A., § 38-604.]

Fornication Law

Idaho Code § 18-6603. Fornication.

Any unmarried person who shall have sexual intercourse with an unmarried person of the opposite sex shall be deemed guilty of fornication, and, upon conviction thereof, shall be punished by a fine of not more than $300 or by imprisonment for not more than six months or by both such fine and imprisonment; provided, that the sentence imposed or any part thereof may be suspended with or without probation in the discretion of the court. [I.C. § 18-6604, as added by 1972, ch. 336, § 1, p. 844.]

Sodomy Law

Idaho Code § 18-6605 (1979):

Every person who is guilty of the infamous crime against nature committed with mankind or with any animal, is punishable by imprisonment in the state prison not less than five years.

ILLINOIS

Fornication Law

Ill. Ann. Stat. § 11-8. Fornication

(a) Any person who cohabits or has sexual intercourse with another not his spouse commits fornication if the behavior is open and notorious.

A person shall be exempt from prosecution under this Section if his liability is based solely on evidence he has given in order to comply with the requirements of Section 4-1.7 of "The Illinois Public Aid Code," approved April 11, 1967, as amended.[1]

(b) Sentence.

Fornication is a Class B misdemeanor.

Ill. Ann. Stat. § 5-1-14. Misdemeanor.

"Misdemeanor" means any offense for which a sentence to a term of imprisonment in other than a penitentiary for less than one year may be imposed.

KANSAS

Sodomy Law

Kan. Stat. Ann. § 21-3505 (1974):

Sodomy is oral or anal copulation between persons who are not husband and wife or consenting adult members of the opposite sex, or between a person and an animal, or coitus with an animal. . . . Sodomy is a class B misdemeanor.

Kan. Stat. Ann. § 21-4502(1)(b) (1974):

For the purposes of sentencing, the following classes of misdemeanors and the punishment and the terms of confinement authorized for each class are established: ... Class B, the sentence of which shall be a definite term of confinement in the county jail which shall be fixed by the court and shall not exceed six (6) months.

Kan. Stat. Ann. § 21-4503(2)(b) (1974):

A person who has been convicted of a misdemeanor may, in addition to or instead of the confinement authorized by law, be sentenced to pay a fine which shall be fixed by the court as follows: ... For a class B misdemeanor, a sum not exceeding $1,000.

KENTUCKY

Sodomy Law

Ky. Rev. Stat. Ann. § 510.100 (Bobbs-Merrill 1975):

(1) A person is guilty of sodomy in the fourth degree when he engages in deviate sexual intercourse with another person of the same sex. (2) Notwithstanding the provisions of KRS 510.020, consent of the other person shall not be a defense under this section, nor shall lack of consent of the other person be an element of this offense. (3) Sodomy in the fourth degree is a Class A misdemeanor.

Ky. Rev. Stat. Ann. § 510.010(1) (Bobbs-Merrill 1975):

"Deviate sexual intercourse" means any act of sexual gratification between persons not married to each other involving the sex organs of one person and the mouth or anus of another.

Ky. Rev. Stat. Ann. § 532.090(1) (Bobbs-Merrill 1982):

A sentence of imprisonment for a misdemeanor shall be a definite term and shall be fixed within the following maximum limitations: ... For a Class A misdemeanor, the term shall not exceed twelve (12) months.

Ky. Rev. Stat. Ann. § 534.040(2)(b) (Bobbs-Merrill 1982):

[A] person who has been convicted of any offense other than a felony may be sentenced to pay a fine in an amount not to exceed: ... For a Class A misdemeanor, $500.

LOUISIANA

Communicable Disease Statutes

La. Rev. Stat. § 1062. Infection of Others Prohibited

It is unlawful for any person to inoculate or infect another person in any manner with a venereal disease or to do any act which will expose another to inoculation or infection with a venereal disease.

La. Rev. Stat. § 1068. Penalty

Whoever violates any provision of this Sub-part or any rule or regulation made hereunder shall, for the first offense, be fined not less than ten dollars nor more than two hundred dollars. For the second offense, he shall be fined not less than twenty-five dollars nor more than four hundred dollars. For each subsequent offense, he shall be find not less than fifty dollars nor more than five hundred dollars or imprisoned for not less than ten days nor more than six months, or both.

Sodomy Law

La. Rev. Stat. § 89. Crime Against Nature

A. Crime against nature is:

(1) The unnatural carnal copulation of a human being with another of the same sex or opposite sex or with an animal, except that anal sexual intercourse between two human beings shall not be deemed as a crime against nature when done under any of the circumstances described in R.S. 14:41, 14:42, 14:42.1 or 14:43. Emission is not necessary; and, when committed by a human being with another, the use of the genital organ of one of the offenders of whatever sex is sufficient to constitute the crime.

(2) The solicitation by a human being of another with the intent to engage in any unnatural carnal copulation for compensation.

B. Whoever violates the provisions of this Section shall be fined not more than two thousand dollars, or imprisoned, with or without hard labor, for not more than five years, or both.

MARYLAND

Sodomy Law

Md. Code Ann. art. 27 §§ 553, 554 (Supp. 1982):

Every person convicted of the crime of sodomy shall be sentenced to the penitentiary for not more than ten years. . . . Every person who is convicted of taking into his or her mouth the sexual organ of any other person or animal, or who shall be convicted of placing his or her sexual organ in the mouth of any other person or animal, or who shall be convicted of committing any other unnatural or perverted sexual practice with any other person or animal, shall be fined not more than one thousand dollars ($1,000.00), or be imprisoned . . . for a period not exceeding ten years (or both). . . .

MASSACHUSETTS

Fornication Law

Mass. Gen. Laws Ann. § 18. Fornication

Whoever commits fornication shall be punished by imprisonment for not more than three months or by a fine of not more than thirty dollars.

MICHIGAN

Fornication Law

Mich. Laws Ann. § 750.335 Lewd and Lascivious Cohabitation and Gross Lewdness

Sec. 335. Any man or woman, not being married to each other, who shall lewdly and lasciviously associate and cohabit together, and any man or woman, married or unmarried, who shall be guilty of open and gross lewdness and lascivious behavior, shall be guilty of a misdemeanor, punishable by imprisonment in the county jail not more than 1 year, or by fine of not more than $500.00. No prosecution shall be commenced under this section after 1 year from the time of committing the offense. As amended P.A.1952, No. 73, § 1, Eff. Sept. 18.

Sodomy Law

Mich. Laws Ann. § 750.158 Penalty

Sec. 158. Any person who shall commit the abominable and detestable crime against nature either with mankind or with any animal shall be guilty of a felony, punishable by imprisonment in the state prison not more than 15 years, or if such person was at the time of the said offense a sexually delinquent person, may be punishable by imprisonment in the state prison for an indeterminate term, the minimum of which shall be 1 day and the maximum of which shall be life. As amended P.A.1952, No. 73, § 1, Eff. Sept. 18.

MINNESOTA

Fornication Law

Minn. Stat. Ann. § 609.34. Fornication

When any man and single woman have sexual intercourse with each other, each is guilty of fornication, which is a misdemeanor.

§ 609.02(3) Misdemeanor.

"Misdemeanor" means a crime for which a sentence of not more than 90 days or a fine of not more than $700, or both, may be imposed.

Sodomy Law

Minn. Stat. Ann. § 609.293. Sodomy

Subdivision 1. Definition. "Sodomy" means carnally knowing any person by the anus or by or with the mouth.
Subds. 2 to 4. Repealed by Laws 1977, c. 130, § 10, eff. May 20, 1977.
Subd. 5. Consensual acts. Whoever, in cases not coming within the provisions of sections 609.342 or 609.344, voluntarily engages in or submits to an act of sodomy with another may be sentenced to imprisonment for not more than one year or to payment of a fine of not more than $3,000, or both. Laws 1967, c. 507, § 4, eff. May 18, 1967. Amended by Laws 1977, c. 130, § 4, eff. May 20, 1977; Laws 1984, c. 628, art. 3, § 11, eff. May 3, 1984.

MISSISSIPPI

Fornication Law

*Miss. Code Ann. § 97-29-1. Adultery and Fornication—
Unlawful Cohabitation.*

If any man and woman shall unlawfully cohabit, whether in adultery or fornication, they shall be fined in any sum not more than five hundred dollars each, and imprisoned in the county jail not more than six months; and it shall not be necessary, to constitute the offense, that the parties shall dwell together publicly as husband and wife, but it may be proved by circumstances which show habitual sexual intercourse.

Sodomy Law

Miss. Code Ann. § 97-29-59. Unnatural Intercourse.

Every person who shall be convicted of the detestable and abominable crime against nature committed with mankind or with a beast, shall be punished by imprisonment in the penitentiary for a term of not more than ten years.

MONTANA

Communicable Disease Statutes

Mont. Code Ann. § 50-18-112. Infected Person Not to Expose Another to Venereal Disease.

A person infected with a venereal disease shall not knowingly expose another person to infection.
History: En. Sec. 97, Ch. 197, L. 1967; R.C.M. 1947, 69-4601(part).

§ 50-18-113. Violation a Misdemeanor.

A person who violates provisions of this chapter or rules adopted by the department of health and environmental sciences concerning venereal disease or who fails or refuses to obey any lawful order issued by a state or local health officer is guilty of a misdemeanor.

Sodomy Law

Mont. Code Ann. § 45-5-505 (1981):

(1) A person who knowingly engages in deviate sexual relations or who causes another to engage in deviate sexual relations commits the offense of deviate sexual conduct.

(2) A person convicted of the offense of deviate sexual conduct shall be imprisoned in the state prison for any term not to exceed 10 years or be fined an amount not to exceed $50,000, or both.

(3) A person convicted of deviate sexual conduct without consent shall be imprisoned in the state prison for any term not to exceed 20 years or be fined an amount not to exceed $50,000, or both.

NEVADA

Communicable Disease Statutes

*Nev. Rev. Stat. Ann. § 202.140 Venereal Diseases: Sexual
Intercourse During Infectious Affliction; Physician
to Report Diseased Prostitute.*

1. Every person afflicted with any infectious or contagious venereal disease which may be conveyed to another, who shall have sexual intercourse with any other person, is guilty of a misdemeanor.

§ 202.150 Exposing Contagious Disease.

Every person afflicted with any infectious or contagious disease, who shall willfully expose himself to another, and any person who shall willfully expose any animal affected with any contagious or infectious disease, in any public place or thoroughfare, except upon his or its necessary removal in a manner not dangerous to the public health or to the health of other animals; and every person so affected who shall willfully expose any other person thereto without his knowledge, shall be guilty of a misdemeanor.

[1911 C&P § 265; RL § 6530; NCL § 10213]

§ 202.160 Bedding Used About Contagious Diseases
Not to Be Reused.

1. Any person who shall knowingly have or use about his premises, or who shall convey, or cause to be conveyed, into any neighborhood, any clothing, bedding, or other substance, used by or in taking care of any person afflicted with smallpox or other infectious or contagious disease, or infected thereby, or shall do any other act with the intent to, or necessarily tending to, spread such disease into any neighborhood or locality, shall be guilty of a misdemeanor.

2. The court trying any such offender may also include in any judgment rendered an order to the effect that the clothing or other property infected be burned or otherwise destroyed, and shall have power to carry such order into effect.

[1911 C&P § 268; RL § 6533; NCL § 10216]-(NRS A 1967, 483)

§ 193.150. Punishment of Misdemeanors.

1. Every person convicted of a misdemeanor shall be punished by imprisonment in the county jail for not more than 6 months, or by a fine of not more than $1,000, or by both fine and imprisonment, unless the statute in

force at the time of commission of such misdemeanor prescribed a different penalty.

2. In lieu of all or a part of the punishment which may be imposed pursuant to subsection 1, if the convicted person agrees, he may be sentenced to perform a fixed period of work for the benefit of the community under the conditions prescribed in NRS 176.087. (C&P 1911, § 20; RL 1912, § 6285; CL 1929, § 9969; 1967, p. 459; 1981, pp. 487, 652.)

Sodomy Law

Nev. Rev. Stat. § 201.190 (1979):

1. Except as provided in NRS 200.366 (sexual assault) and 201.230 (lewdness with a child), every person of full age who commits the infamous crime against nature shall be punished by imprisonment in the state prison for not less than 1 year nor more than 6 years.

2. The "infamous crime against nature" means anal intercourse, cunnilingus or fellatio between consenting adults of the same sex.

NEW JERSEY

Communicable Disease Statutes

N.J. Stat. Ann. § 26:4-42. Occupations Forbidden Infected Persons

No person having a venereal disease in the infectious stage shall:

a. Engage in the nursing or care of children or of the sick;

b. Engage in the preparation, manufacture or handling of milk, milk products or other foodstuffs;

c. Work or be permitted to work in any dairy, creamery, milk depot or other place where milk or its products are produced, manufactured or sold, or in any other establishment where foods are exposed or handled;

d. Engage in any other occupation of such a nature that his infection may be transmitted to others; or

e. Conduct himself in such a manner as to expose others to infection.

§ 26:4-129. Liability to Penalties in General

Except as otherwise specifically provided in this chapter, a person who violates any of the provisions of this chapter, or fails to perform any duty imposed by this chapter at the time and in the manner provided, shall be liable to a penalty of not less than ten nor more than one hundred dollars for each offense.

NEW YORK

Communicable Disease Statutes

McKinney's Consolidated Laws of New York § 2307. Venereal Disease; Person Knowing Himself to Be Infected

Any person who, knowing himself or herself to be infected with an infectious venereal disease, has sexual intercourse with another shall be guilty of a misdemeanor.

§ 80.051 Fines for Misdemeanors and Violation

1. Class A misdemeanor. A sentence to pay a fine for a class A misdemeanor shall be a sentence to pay an amount, fixed by the court, not exceeding one thousand dollars, provided, however, that a sentence imposed for a violation of section 215.80 of this chapter may include a fine in an amount equivalent to double the value of the property unlawfully disposed of in the commission of the crime.

2. Class B misdemeanor. A sentence to pay a fine for a class B misdemeanor shall be a sentence to pay an amount, fixed by the court, not exceeding five hundred dollars.

3. Unclassified misdemeanor. A sentence to pay a fine for an unclassified misdemeanor shall be a sentence to pay an amount, fixed by the court, in accordance with the provisions of the law or ordinance that defines the crime.

4. "Misdemeanor" means an offense, other than a "traffic infraction," for which a sentence to a term of imprisonment in excess of fifteen days may be imposed, but for which a sentence to a term of imprisonment in excess of one year cannot be imposed.

NORTH CAROLINA

Fornication Law

N.C. Gen. Stat. § 14-184. Fornication and Adultery.

If any man and woman, not being married to each other, shall lewdly and lasciviously associate, bed and cohabit together, they shall be guilty of a misdemeanor: Provided, that the admissions or confessions of one shall not be received in evidence against the other. Any person violating any provision of this section shall be punishable by a fine not to exceed five hundred dollars ($500.00), imprisonment for not more than six months, or both. (1805, c. 684, P.R.; R.C., c. 34, s. 45; Code, s. 1041; Rev., s. 3350; C.S., s. 4343; 1969, c. 1224, s. 9.)

Sodomy Law

N.C. Gen. Stat. § 14-177 (1981):

If any person shall commit the crime against nature, with mankind or beast, he shall be punished as a Class H felony.

N.C. Gen. Stat. § 14-1.1(a)(8) (1981):

For felonies that occur on or after ... [July 1, 1981] ... the following punishments shall be applicable: ... A Class H felony shall be punishable by imprisonment up to 10 years, or a fine or both.

NORTH DAKOTA

Communicable Disease Statute

N.D. Cent. Code § 23-07-21. Penalties.

Any person:

1. Who violates or fails to obey any of the provisions of this chapter, any lawful rule or regulation made by the state department of health, or any order issued by any state, county, or municipal health officer;

2. Who violates any quarantine law or regulation, or who leaves a quarantined area without being discharged; or

3. Who, knowing that he is infected with a venereal disease, willfully exposes another person to infection, is guilty of an infraction. (Class B misdemeanor, punishable by a maximum penalty of 30 days imprisonment and/or a fine of $500.)

Fornication Law

N.D. Cent. Code § 12.1-20-12. Deviate Sexual Act.

A person who performs a deviate sexual act with the intent to arouse or gratify his sexual desire is guilty of a class A misdemeanor.

§ 12.1-32-01(5)

Class A misdemeanor, for which a maximum penalty of one year's imprisonment, a fine of one thousand dollars, or both, may be imposed.

OKLAHOMA

Communicable Disease Statute

Okla. Stat. Ann. § 1-519. Diseased Persons—Marriage or Sexual Intercourse

It shall be unlawful and a felony for any person, after becoming an infected person and before being discharged and pronounced cured by a physician in writing, to marry any other person, or to expose any other person by the act of copulation or sexual intercourse to such venereal disease or to liability to contract the same. Laws 1963, c. 325, art. 5, § 519.

Sodomy Law

Okla. Stat. Ann. tit. 21. § 886 (West 1983):

Every person who is guilty of the detestable and abominable crime against nature, committed with mankind or with a beast, is punishable by imprisonment in the penitentiary not exceeding ten (10) years.

OREGON

Communicable Disease Statutes

Oreg. Rev. Stat. Ann. § 434.180 Conduct and Occupations of Infected Persons Restricted.

No person having any venereal disease in the infectious stage shall:
(1) Conduct himself in such a manner as to expose others to infection.
(2) Engage in the nursing or care of children or of the sick, or in any other occupation of such a nature that the infection may be transmitted to others. [Amended by 1973 c. 829 § 46]

§ 161.615 Prison Terms for Misdemeanors.

Sentences for misdemeanors shall be for a definite term. The court shall fix the term of imprisonment within the following maximum limitations:
(1) For a Class A misdemeanor, 1 year.
(2) For a Class B misdemeanor, 6 months.
(3) For a Class C misdemeanor, 30 days.
(4) For an unclassified misdemeanor, as provided in the statute defining the crime. [1971 c. 743]

§ 161.635 Fines for Misdemeanors and Violations.

(1) A sentence to pay a fine for a misdemeanor shall be a sentence to pay an amount, fixed by the court, not exceeding:

(a) $2,500 for a Class A misdemeanor.

(b) $1,000 for a Class B misdemeanor.

(c) $500 for a Class C misdemeanor.

(2) A sentence to pay a fine for an unclassified misdemeanor shall be a sentence to pay an amount, fixed by the court, as provided in the statute defining the crime.

(3) A sentence to pay a fine for a violation shall be a sentence to pay an amount, fixed by the court, not exceeding $250.

PENNSYLVANIA

Fornication Law

Penn. Stat. Ann. § 3124. Voluntary Deviate Sexual Intercourse

A person who engages in deviate sexual intercourse under circumstances not covered by section 3123 of this title (related to involuntary deviate sexual intercourse) is guilty of a misdemeanor of the second degree.

RHODE ISLAND

Communicable Disease Statute

R.I. Gen. Laws § 23-11-1. Diseases Declared Contagious—
Exposure of Another to Infection.

Sexually transmitted diseases shall include but not be limited to syphilis, gonorrhea, chancroid, granuloma inguinale and lymphogranuloma venereum and such other diseases as the director of the department of health may by regulation determine to constitute a sexually transmitted disease. Sexually transmitted diseases are hereby declared to be contagious, infectious, communicable and dangerous to the public health. It shall be unlawful for anyone knowingly, while in the infectious condition with these diseases, or any of them, to expose another person to infection. Any person found guilty of violating the provisions of this section shall be fined not more than one hundred dollars ($100) or imprisoned for not more than three (3) months.

Fornication Law

R.I. Gen. Laws § 11-34-5. Transportation for Indecent Purposes— Harboring Prostitution.

It shall be unlawful for any person, for pecuniary gain, to secure, direct or transport, or offer to secure, direct or transport another for the purpose of prostitution, or for any other lewd or indecent act; or to receive or offer or agree to receive any person into any place, structure, house, building, room, or conveyance for the purpose of committing any such acts, or knowingly permit any person to remain therein for any such purposes, or to, in any way, aid or abet or participate in any of the acts or things enumerated herein.

Any person found guilty under this section, shall be subject to imprisonment in the adult correctional institutions not to exceed five (5) years.

Sodomy Law

R.I. Gen. Laws § 11-10-1 (Replacement 1969):

Every person who shall be convicted of the abominable and detestable crime against nature, either with mankind or with any beast, shall be imprisoned not exceeding twenty (20) years nor less than seven (7) years.

SOUTH CAROLINA

Communicable Disease Statutes

S.C. Code Ann. § 44-29-60. Venereal Diseases Declared Dangerous to Public Health; Infection of Another with Venereal Disease.

Syphilis, gonorrhea and chancroid, hereinafter designated as venereal diseases, are hereby declared to be contagious, infectious, communicable and dangerous to the public health. It shall be unlawful for anyone infected with these diseases, or any of them, to expose another to infection.

S.C. Code Ann. § 44-29-140. Penalties Pertaining to Venereal Disease.

Any person who shall violate any of the provisions of §§ 44-29-60 to 44-29-140, other than § 44-29-120, or any lawful rule or regulation made by the Department of Health and Environmental Control pursuant to the authority herein granted, or pursuant to the authority granted by any other statute law, or shall fail or refuse to obey any lawful order issued by any State, county or municipal health officer, pursuant to the authority granted in §§ 44-29-60 to 44-29-140, or any other law or the regulations prescribed thereunder, shall be guilty of a misdemeanor and, upon conviction thereof by any court of competent jurisdiction, shall be fined not more than twenty dollars or be imprisoned for not more than twenty days.

Fornication Law

S.C. Code Ann. § 16-15-60. Adultery or Fornication.

Any man or woman who shall be guilty of the crime of adultery or fornication shall be liable to indictment and, on conviction, shall be severally punished by a fine of not less than one hundred dollars nor more than five hundred dollars or imprisonment for not less than six months nor more than one year or by both fine and imprisonment, at the discretion of the court.

§ 16-15-80. "Fornication" Defined.

"Fornication" is the living together and carnal intercourse with each other or habitual carnal intercourse with each other without living together of a man and woman, both being unmarried.

Sodomy Law

S.C. Code Ann. § 16-15-120 (Law. Co-op. 1977):

Whoever shall commit the abominable crime of buggery, whether with mankind or with beast, shall, on conviction, be guilty of felony and shall be imprisoned in the Penitentiary for five years or shall pay a fine of not less than five hundred dollars, or both, at the discretion of the court.

SOUTH DAKOTA

Communicable Disease Statutes

S.D. Code § 34-23-1. Diseases Declared Dangerous—Exposure of Another as Misdemeanor.

Syphilis, gonorrhea, and chancroid hereinafter designated as venereal diseases are hereby declared to be contagious, infectious, communicable, and dangerous to the public health. It is a Class 2 misdemeanor for anyone infected with these diseases or any of them to expose another person to infection.

§ 22-6-3

(2) Class 2 misdemeanor: thirty days imprisonment in a county jail or one hundred dollars fine, or both.

Except in cases where punishment is prescribed by law, every offense declared to be a misdemeanor and not otherwise classified, is a Class 1 misdemeanor.

Where the performance of an act is prohibited by a statute, and no penalty for the violation of such statute is imposed by a statute, the doing of such act is a Class 2 misdemeanor.

TENNESSEE

Communicable Disease Statutes

Tenn. Code Ann. § 68-10-107. Exposure of Others by Infected Person.

It shall be a violation of this chapter for any person infected with a venereal disease to expose another person to such infection. [Acts 1921, ch. 106, § 8; Shan. Supp., § 3116a15; Code 1932, § 5820; T.C.A. (orig. ed.), § 53-1107.]

Tenn. Code Ann. § 68-10-111. Violation of Chapter—Penalty.

Any health officer or any other person who fails to perform the duties required of him in this chapter, or violates any of the provisions of same, or of any rule or bylaw promulgated under its authority, shall be guilty of a misdemeanor, and be fined not less than twenty-five dollars ($25.00) and not more than five hundred dollars ($500), and each violation shall be a separate offense. [Acts 1921, ch. 106, § 12; Shan. Supp., § 3116a19; mod. Code 1932, § 5824; T.C.A. (orig. ed.), § 53-1111.]

Sodomy Law

Tenn. Code Ann. § 39-2-612 (1982):

Crimes against nature, either with mankind or any beast, are punishable by imprisonment in the penitentiary not less than five (5) nor more than fifteen (15) years.

TEXAS

Communicable Disease Statutes

Texas Penal Code Ann. § 6.01. (Vernon):

(a) A person commits an offense if the person knowingly exposes another person to infection with a reportable venereal disease.

(b) An offense under this section is a Class B misdemeanor.

§ 12.22. Class B Misdemeanor

An individual adjudged guilty of a Class B misdemeanor shall be punished by:

(1) a fine not to exceed $1,000;

(2) confinement in jail for a term not to exceed 180 days; or

(3) both such fine and imprisonment.

Sodomy Law

Tex. Penal Code Ann. § 21.06 (Vernon 1974):

(a) A person commits an offense if he engages in deviate sexual intercourse with another individual of the same sex.

(b) An offense under the section is a Class C misdemeanor.

Tex. Penal Code Ann. § 12.01 (Vernon 1974):

"Deviate sexual intercourse" means . . . any contact with any part of the genitals of one person and the mouth or anus of another person.

Tex. Penal Code Ann. § 12.23 (Vernon 1974):

An individual adjudged guilty of a Class C misdemeanor shall be punished by a fine not to exceed $200.

UTAH

Communicable Disease Statutes

Utah Code Ann. § 26-6-5. Willful Introduction of Communicable Disease a Misdemeanor.

Any person who willfully or knowingly introduces any communicable or infectious disease into any county, municipality, or community is guilty of a class A misdemeanor.

Utah Code Ann. § 76-3-302 (Penalties)

One thousand dollars when the conviction is of a class A misdemeanor; (or imprisonment not to exceed one year).

Fornication Law

Utah Code Ann. § 76-7-104. Fornication

(1) Any unmarried person who shall voluntarily engage in sexual intercourse with another is guilty of fornication.

(2) Fornication is a class B misdemeanor.

Sodomy Law

Utah Code Ann. § 76-5-403 (1983):

(1) A person commits sodomy when the actor engages in any sexual act with a person who is 14 years of age or older involving the genitals of one person and mouth or anus of another person, regardless of the sex of either participant.

(2) A person commits forcible sodomy when the actor commits sodomy upon another without the other's consent.

(3) Sodomy is a class B misdemeanor. Forcible sodomy is a felony of the first degree.

Utah Code Ann. § 76-3-204 (1978):

A person who has been convicted of a misdemeanor may be sentenced to imprisonment as follows: . . . In the case of a class B misdemeanor, for a term not exceeding six months.

VERMONT

Communicable Disease Statute

Vt. Stat. Ann. § 1106. Sexual Intercourse When Infected with Venereal Disease

A person who has sexual intercourse while knowingly infected with gonorrhea or syphilis in a communicable stage shall be imprisoned not more than two years or fined not more than $500.00, or both.—Amended 1973, No. 89, § 11; 1981, No. 223 (Adj. Sess.), § 23.

VIRGINIA

Fornication Law

Va. Code § 18.2-344. Fornication.

Any person, not being married, who voluntarily shall have sexual intercourse with any other person, shall be guilty of fornication, punishable as a Class 4 misdemeanor. (Code 1950, §§ 18.1-188, 18.1-190; 1960, c. 358; 1975, cc. 14, 15.)

Va. Code § 18.2-11. Punishment for Conviction of Misdemeanor.

The authorized punishments for conviction of a misdemeanor are:

(a) For Class 1 misdemeanors, confinement in jail for not more than twelve months and a fine of not more than $1,000, either or both.

(b) For Class 2 misdemeanors, confinement in jail for not more than six months and a fine of not more than $500, either or both.

(c) For Class 3 misdemeanors, a fine of not more than $500.

(d) For Class 4 misdemeanors, a fine of not more than $100. (1975, cc. 14, 15.)

Sodomy Law

Va. Code § 18.2-361 (1982):

If any person shall carnally know in any manner any brute animal, or carnally know any male or female person by the anus or by or with the mouth, or voluntarily submit to such carnal knowledge, he or she shall be guilty of a Class 6 felony.

Va. Code § 18.2-10 (1982):

The authorized punishments for conviction of a felony are: . . . For Class 6 felonies, a term of imprisonment of not less than one year nor more than five years, or in the discretion of the jury or the court trying the case without a jury, confinement in jail for not more than twelve months and a fine of not more than $1,000, either or both.

WASHINGTON

Communicable Disease Statutes

Wash. Rev. Code § 70.24.010 (West):
Venereal Diseases Designated.

Syphilis, gonorrhea and chancroid hereinafter designated as venereal diseases are hereby declared to be contagious, infectious, communicable and dangerous to the public health. It shall be unlawful for anyone infected with these diseases or any of them to expose another person to infection.

Wash. Rev. Code § 70.24.040 (West):
Rules and Regulations—Penalty.

The state board of health is hereby empowered and directed to make such rules and regulations as shall in its judgment be necessary for the carrying out of the provisions of this act, including rules and regulations providing for the control and treatment of persons isolated or quarantined under the provisions of RCW 70.24.020, and such other rules and regulations, not in conflict with provisions of this act, concerning the control of venereal diseases, and concerning the care, treatment and quarantine of persons infected therewith, as it may from time to time deem advisable. All such rules and regulations so made shall be of force and binding upon all county and municipal health officers and other persons affected by this act, and shall have the force and effect of law: *Provided,* That such regulations shall prescribe reasonable safeguards against the disclosure of the names of any such infected persons, who faithfully comply with the provisions of this act and the lawful regulations of the state board of health, except to officers and physicians charged with the enforcement of this act and such rules and regulations and any violation of such safeguarding regulations, shall be a gross misdemeanor.

Wash. Rev. Code § 9.92.020. (West): Punishment of Gross
Misdemeanor When Not Fixed by Statute

Every person convicted of a gross misdemeanor for which no punishment is prescribed in any statute in force at the time of conviction and sentence, shall be punished by imprisonment in the county jail for a maximum term fixed by the court of not more than one year, or by a fine in an amount fixed by the court of not more than five thousand dollars, or by both such imprisonment and fine.

WEST VIRGINIA

Fornication Law

W. Va. Code § 61-8-3. Adultery and Fornication; Penalty.

If any person commit adultery or fornication, he shall be guilty of a misdemeanor, and, upon conviction, shall be fined not less than twenty dollars. (Code 1849, c. 196, § 6; Code 1860, c. 196, § 6; Code 1868, c. 149, § 6; Code 1882, c. 123, § 6; Code 1923, c. 149, § 6.)

WISCONSIN

Fornication Law

Wis. Stat. Ann. § 944.15 (West): Fornication

(1) In this section, "in public" means in a place where or in a manner such that the person knows or has reason to know that his or her conduct is observable by or in the presence of persons other than the person with whom he or she is having sexual intercourse.

(2) Whoever has sexual intercourse in public or whoever has sexual intercourse with a minor who is 16 years old or older but younger than 18 years old and who is not his or her spouse is guilty of a Class * * * A misdemeanor.

Sodomy Law

Wis. Stat. Ann. § 944.17 (West 1982):

Whoever does either of the following is guilty of a Class A misdemeanor:

(1) Commits an abnormal act of sexual gratification involving the sex organ of one person and the mouth or anus of another or

(2) Commits an act of sexual gratification involving his sex organ and the sex organ, mouth or anus of an animal

Wis. Stat. Ann. § 939.51 (West 1982):

Penalties for misdemeanors are as follows: . . . For a Class A misdemeanor, a fine of not to exceed $10,000 or imprisonment not to exceed 9 months, or both.

WYOMING

Communicable Disease Statutes

Wyo. Stat. Ann. § 35-4-109

Any person who shall knowingly have or use about his premises, or who shall convey or cause to be conveyed into any neighborhood, any clothing, bedding, or other substance used by, or in taking care of, any person afflicted with the smallpox or other infectious or contagious disease, or infected thereby, or shall do any other act with intent to, or necessarily tending to the spread of such disease into any neighborhood or locality, shall be deemed guilty of a misdemeanor and upon conviction thereof before any court of competent jurisdiction shall be fined in any sum not more than five hundred dollars ($500.00) or imprisoned in the county jail not exceeding six (6) months, or by both fine and imprisonment; and the court trying any such offender may also include arraignment rendered, an order to the effect that the clothing or other property infected be burned or otherwise destroyed, and shall have power to carry such order into effect.

Wyo. Stat. Ann. § 35-4-110: Same; Liability for Damages in Civil Action

Any person guilty of violating the provisions of section one of this act (Sect. 35-4-109) in addition to the penalties therein prescribed, shall be liable in a civil action in damages to any and all persons, who may, from that cause, become infected with such contagious disease; said damages shall be so assessed as to include in addition to other damages, all expenses incurred by reason of such sickness, loss of time and burial expenses; and such action may also be maintained by the representative of any deceased person.

Index

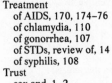